More Praise for *The Business of Family*

"*The Business of Family* is an easy-to-read primer on how to put 'family first' through communication and commitment. Linda Davis Taylor writes, 'Money can either unite or divide us. The money doesn't decide. We do.' Linda guides the reader in using business principles to keep the family—and its values—intact."

—CAROL A. JOHNSTON,
Partner in Trusts and Estates
at Katten Muchin Rosenman LLP

"Linda Davis Taylor shows you how to blend business experience, strategic planning, conflict resolution, and investment advice into a package that will take your family assets to the next generation and beyond. A longtime investment and family adviser, Taylor offers practical advice and wisdom on how to manage the wealth and well-being of our families. A 'must' read for every family with enough money to pass some on to the next generation."

—JOHN BARKAI,
Professor of Law and Director of Clinical Programs,
University of Hawaii Law School

"Provides superb strategies to families seeking to instill appreciation for their resources and to ensure that succeeding generations will manage those resources wisely. I found her suggestions for creating a sense of philanthropic responsibility particularly engaging. This is a sophisticated plan for promoting multi-generational fiscal responsibility, philanthropic inclination and family harmony."

—SCOTT H. BICE, ROBERT C. AND NANNETTE P. PACKARD
Professor of Law,
University of Southern California

The Business of Family
How to Stay Rich for Generations

Linda Davis Taylor

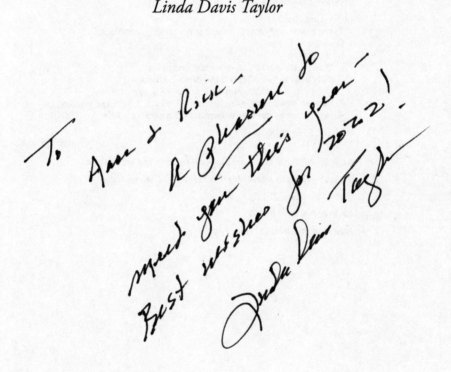

To Ann & Rose –

A pleasure to meet you this year –

Best wishes for 2022!

Linda Davis Taylor

palgrave
macmillan

THE BUSINESS OF FAMILY
Copyright © Linda Davis Taylor, 2015.

First published in 2015 by
PALGRAVE MACMILLAN®
in the United States—a division of St. Martin's Press LLC,
175 Fifth Avenue, New York, NY 10010.

Where this book is distributed in the UK, Europe and the rest of the world,
this is by Palgrave Macmillan, a division of Macmillan Publishers Limited,
registered in England, company number 785998, of Houndmills,
Basingstoke, Hampshire RG21 6XS.

Palgrave Macmillan is the global academic imprint of the above companies
and has companies and representatives throughout the world.

Palgrave® and Macmillan® are registered trademarks in the United States,
the United Kingdom, Europe and other countries.

ISBN: 978–1–137–48786–5

Library of Congress Cataloging-in-Publication Data

Taylor, Linda Davis.
    The business of family : how to stay rich for generations /
Linda Davis Taylor.
        pages cm
    Includes bibliographical references and index.
    ISBN 978–1–137–48786–5 (hardcover : alk. paper)
        1. Family-owned business enterprises—Management.
    2. Family-owned business enterprises—Finance. 3. Strategic planning.
    4. Family-owned business enterprises—Succession. I. Title.

HD62.25.T359 2015
332.024'01—dc23   2014047351

A catalogue record of the book is available from the British Library.

Design by Newgen Knowledge Works (P) Ltd., Chennai, India.

First edition: June 2015

10 9 8 7 6 5 4 3 2 1

Printed in the United States of America.

Contents

Staying on Track

Long-Term Planning

Figures

Foreword

Business and family are the two most important entrepreneurial institutions in the world. To build either of them successfully requires tremendous commitment, energy, and focus. If all goes well, the founders will have something of value to pass on to future generations.

When I was a young man, I knew I wanted to succeed at two things. The first was to build a significant family. Having adequate resources would make this much easier to do, so I also wanted to do well in business.

Sixty years later, I am grateful to have accomplished both of the goals I set out to achieve. Our third generation is launched and thriving. They're doing things differently from my generation, and they're doing well. The goal was to provide them with the encouragement and skills to put their own stamp on things. I founded three successful businesses, the fruits of which have allowed us to support our families and to give back to the communities that provided us with so much opportunity. I believe it's important to be grateful.

As an investment counselor for over fifty years, I have studied with admiration the entrepreneurial successes and failures of companies. I've spent my business career advising families how to build their own capital by investing in great companies. In my opinion, the combination of the two—business and family—is a natural. As the years went on, my interest in family issues deepened. I discovered that the difference between a good outcome and a truly great outcome lies in the family relationships and the decisions families make.

My other great interest is in education. It's what can really give people a leg up as they get to work on making their lives a success. It was in the education setting where I met Linda Davis Taylor. We have been colleagues for nearly 25 years as trustees at Scripps College, business associates, and close friends.

Linda and I share the belief that families are the most important businesses of all. We've counseled one another on every significant business and family issue there is. About a decade ago, at Linda's suggestion, we began having regular family meetings. At first, they were very simple undertakings. We would spend an hour or two in my office with my immediate family to review important and sometimes not so important items of the day.

Our family meetings have continued. And they've evolved. We've done many of the things Linda suggests in her book, including financial education, philanthropy, and succession planning. I'm at the stage of life where legacy is quite important. I want to make sure I do everything I can to pass on wealth. Money is one kind, of course. But the greatest wealth is found in family.

That's why this is a truly important book.

PHILIP V. SWAN

Acknowledgments

The inspiration for this book has come from families.

First and foremost, of course, is my extended family, those who came before me and paved the way, and those who have loved and guided me through my journey. My wonderful husband and best friend, Jim Taylor, gave me steady encouragement, astute comments, and most of all, time and patience. Our amazing daughters, Della and Katie, have been my best cheering section since day one. I know our family's future will be in good hands with them.

Hundreds of families contributed to this project. This didn't happen through a formal research process, but over many years of sharing their experiences, challenges, and ideas about how to build and sustain successful families. I am grateful to each of them for the gift of being a small part of their family's path.

My professional colleagues in business, education, and philanthropy provided insights, wisdom, and unfailing support. They supported my passion. They are my family of mentors and friends.

The expertise and guidance of a superb editorial team actually made this project a reality. Laurie Harting, Cynthia Zigmund, Brett Block, and John and Lisa Barclay placed their confidence in me and never wavered.

Thank you and good luck to all of you who are committed to the business of family.

Introduction

How do families build and maintain their wealth? This question has challenged families for generations. In business, any wise entrepreneur would develop a plan to guide the venture. Though most people don't have a strategy in mind for their families, that is precisely what they need. This book applies business concepts to investment in our families with as much focus and discipline as we do for investment in our financial assets.

As the CEO of the nation's oldest investment advisory firm, Clifford Swan Investment Counsel, I've seen firsthand how important it is for the family to be connected by a common purpose. With an unprecedented amount of wealth passing to the next generation, the opportunity exists to reverse the old "shirtsleeves to shirtsleeves in three generations" proverb. Applying a business mind-set to the family strategy will help families do that.

First Things First

Starting a new business takes more than a dream. Business people have a plan. From financing to manufacturing to sales, owners pour in sweat equity as well as financial equity. Building a successful family requires the same well-thought-out strategy.

A business without a plan won't be in business for long. A family without a plan may be around for a while, but will it prosper and thrive? Nobody sets out simply to break even. You need profits to stay afloat. For a family, those go beyond money. By using the same winning ideas that successful companies employ, your family can reap benefits that will keep you in the black.

A company needs a dynamic vision in order to be competitive in today's marketplace. For a business, this is the drive that's sewn into the very fabric of the organization. Once established, it allows every employee to understand the company's ambitions. For a family, a vision is what keeps everyone working together, even in challenging times.

Financial circumstances can change. Jobs come and go. Illness may strike. Divorce happens. When problems arise, family members must be just as unified around a common purpose as members are in a business.

"Family values" is a phrase so common that we assume we know what they are. But do we? Companies are now including values in their strategies and business schools are big on ethics classes. "Value" is a buzzword with a dual meaning, but the true definition remains elusive. From Enron to Madoff to the recent financial collapse, it's clear that earnings have to be grounded in reality to stand the test of time.

Insider trading is the ultimate financial crime. However, family values that are frittered away can do generations of harm. Defining values and practicing them is a strategy every family can use to prevent anybody from taking a shortcut that doesn't pay.

Getting Your Family on Board

Collaboration and teamwork are the new axioms for business success. Firms vie for a spot on the "Best Places to Work" lists because happy employees make productive employees. Company loyalty can't be taken for granted anymore, so companies invest to retain the brightest people.

Businesses develop their people and strive for goals where everyone has something to gain. A family that identifies and utilizes each member's strengths lays a foundation of trust and communication, the two most crucial ingredients for working together well. All families face problems, as do all businesses. Those that forge real partnerships with their people will prosper.

Whether it's a company revenue target or an IPO, a family vacation or a family vision, having goals that are specific, realistic, and inspiring creates enthusiasm and optimism. The mission sets people on course. The goals get them there.

With a purpose defined and milestones set, the family has a head start on becoming a winning team. Small accomplishments lead to bigger ones. One set of goals leads to the next, and the seeds of success are sown.

Good results are a product of clear direction, and everybody doing his or her part. From the sales team to the C-suite, each employee in a company has a role. A family also needs schedules and duties assigned to organize the whirlwind of activity into meaningful progress. Someone has to make the calls on who's doing what and why.

Even when everybody understands what he or she is supposed to do and why, problems still crop up. If things go off the rails at work, results suffer until the issue is fixed. When this happens at home, we need a warning light to get us back on track. Working together toward common goals makes mid-course corrections much easier.

Investing in the People

Upper-level management wouldn't turn over important responsibilities to new employees without making sure they had the skills and training for the jobs. Performance is reviewed. Budgets are scrutinized. But families often take this gamble because financial education is frequently ignored.

We teach our kids academic skills and athletic skills, yet money skills remain lacking. From the Internet to debit cards, it only takes an instant to make a bad financial decision. For parents, educating their children about money isn't simply about getting a small return on their cash but generations of returns.

It's never been easier to connect and communicate with family members. From smartphones to e-mails to Skype, our loved ones are only a click away. The challenge is communicating well when it comes to important matters, especially money.

A smart company would never have just one "make it or break it" meeting to relay its objectives to employees. Be it at work or at home, financial matters can rarely be summed up in a matter of minutes. Money talks shouldn't be treated like texts. Though they can be short and to the point, they require some time and effort. Families need more than a "shared data" plan. They need a shared strategy that really pays off.

In business, the role of mentors in passing on corporate wisdom is a priceless asset. In a family, mentorship is equally essential. Handing down history and insight from one generation to the next is smart HR for the family.

Company leaders develop their employees for the future with an objective in sight. They fund workshops, advanced degrees, and specialized training to keep their people on the cutting edge. Families have a built-in talent pool, an often overlooked and untapped resource. This is the best kind of capital there is—the human kind.

Staying on Track

Meetings are a mainstay at the office. From mom-and-pop businesses to global corporations, firms need them to preserve productivity and sustain the flow of information in a fast-paced world. Even if the family version of a business meeting is in the living room rather than the boardroom, a regular gathering will keep confusion low and morale high.

From the family calendar to family finances, including everyone in the discussion keeps the mystery out of how important decisions are made. It's a forum for conversation, information, and solving problems. Whether it's a daily check-in or an annual retreat, family meetings are where the business of the family happens.

Businesses focus on the bottom line. Nobody blushes during frank company budget talks. That's not always the case when men and women return home, and they're off the clock. Earnings, spending, and savings are line items a family can't ignore. At work, sustainability hinges on taking care of profits as well as employees to guarantee resiliency over time. A family has to conserve for the future too. Making finances a little more human and family a little more corporate in dealing with money is a winning formula for staying rich.

The wealthy know their family and their money aren't mutually exclusive. Though they may pay someone to do the spending reports for them, they educate their entire family about money. This same principle will work for any family, even if their version of a family office is the computer in the family room.

Today's technology allows every family to have a hub for its operations. The phrase "home office" will have more meaning when every member of the family can access it, provide input, and unite around shared goals. In whatever form, a family office helps the family focus on its future.

Long-Term Planning

The best companies appreciate that giving back to their communities goes beyond the tax write-off. Families that give and make it about more than cutting a check earn extra dividends too, keeping everybody grateful and grounded. Working together for a common cause teaches financial skills and foments a sense of purpose. Families built on values rather than fortunes are destined to endure.

Whether you're in a corporation or a family, success is not guaranteed. The research and development division of a firm is dedicated to investigating new ideas and cultivating them so the business continues to grow. R&D is about spending now to produce revenue later. A company that invests in itself to fuel its future sales keeps its profits high.

Whether it's saving for college to educate the next generation or saving for a trip so the family can spend quality time together, investing for the future is about more than having a savings account. Family membership evolves. As it does, the members bring new skills, talents, and ideas to the table. This is growth potential for the family, and it needs to be nurtured.

Businesses accept that their employees won't work there forever. Retirement is something they plan for. In a family, there is no success without succession.

Once the mission is crafted and the values are clear, the cherished family stories need to be told. Although the family may have a financial estate plan set up, the members need an emotional one too.

* * *

Understanding how to run a successful business isn't all that different from understanding how to run a successful family. Just like a company, a family must invest in its people who require support, training, and commitment to a purpose. Just like a company, a family deals with unexpected challenges but never forgets to celebrate its milestones. Just like a company, a family needs laser-sharp focus on its goals in order to thrive.

Why haven't families put such plans in place? Because we haven't been shown how to.

If the answer to maintaining wealth were easy, the old "shirtsleeves to shirtsleeves in three generations" problem would have disappeared long ago. Families and money are complicated even when they're not together. *The Business of Family* shows you how to reframe the old business adage about working smart rather than hard.

The Business of Family is not a business book about how to make money. *The Business of Family* is about the most important business of all—your family.

First Things First

CHAPTER 1

Strategy: A Blueprint for Your Family

There are over 9 million households in the United States worth at least $1 million. This number grew by over 600,000 in 2013 alone. Let's be honest, if we have money, we want to hold on to it. And if we haven't yet made it, we're working hard to reach our magic number. To get there, we need to make sure we have a family plan that's as strong as our financial plan.

Over 70 percent of wealth doesn't last beyond three generations. That means making the money isn't the only problem. Keeping it is just as challenging.

Whether our family succeeds depends as much on what we do as on what our investments do. This isn't the "soft stuff" as so many financial experts say. It's the hard stuff. A family's business is about a whole lot more than money.

After years of counseling affluent families on their finances, I thought I had a firm grasp on the relationship between family members and money. That was until my father's eightieth birthday. As my siblings and I gathered for a casual dinner to celebrate, Dad told us about leaving his southern town on a freight train in search of something better. It was the first time he'd ever mentioned this pivotal moment. We had never talked with our parents about what motivated them to do all they had done, or what we—the next generation—wanted to do with their legacy. A year later, both of our parents were gone, and we had missed a priceless opportunity. I realized that the "business of the family" had yet to embrace the secrets that actual businesses know by heart.

Sooner than we can imagine we find ourselves as the grown-ups, parents aging and passing on. Do we understand what they stood for? Do our kids have a sense of the family's history? Will our grandkids be connected enough to care?

Billionaires beginning with the Rockefellers set up family offices to do nothing but run their affairs. This same principle will work for any family, even if their version of a corner office is a laptop in the corner of their kitchen. Every family needs its own business plan to ensure its members know where they've been, where they're going, and how they are going to get there.

Study after study shows that it takes good plans as well as good habits to succeed in business. Private companies make up 99 percent of all firms in the United States. In 2012, these businesses grew twice as fast as public companies in the Standard & Poor's 500 index. A *Forbes* analysis has suggested that successful firms like these have six strategies that contribute to their superior results.[1]

What exactly do these companies have in common?

1. They have a clear mission. If they lose focus, they will ultimately lose money.
2. They take good care of their employees because people are their biggest asset.
3. They are willing to adapt and change in order to remain competitive.
4. They make decisions with long-term results in mind, not just short-term gains.
5. They look outside their own walls so their thinking doesn't get stale.
6. Over half of these firms are still family-owned, and they have a strategy for the family as well as for the business.

While we don't often link business success to family success, this last statistic proves that it is a readily transferable model. Thinking like an owner—whether in a business or a family—is a winning formula. We all can use time-tested business model methods to make our families run better.

Sweet Success

Who would have thought that one of America's most successful families started their business with only $400 while working out of a one-room apartment above a candy factory in Minneapolis? Mars is famous for making delicious candy, but the family credits its real success to solid principles learned early on at home. They stayed out of debt—both the literal and the emotional kind—by focusing on goals to unite them for enduring profitability. They also kept a close eye on their personal bottom line, which was built on values rather than fortunes.

Forrest Mars Sr. was the only son of Ethel M. and Frank C. Mars, a lackluster candy salesman. Frank's Mar-O-Bar Company was only modestly successful at first. It was his son Forrest's idea to make a malt-flavored nougat bar named Milky Way. His new idea turned the tide. When Forrest took over the company after his father died, his strong sense of personal responsibility, discipline, and frugality influenced his business principles.

Based on Forrest's values, these five principles became the company credo:

1. Quality
2. Responsibility
3. Mutuality
4. Efficiency
5. Freedom

He taught this philosophy to his kids as well. Like their father, the Mars children worked for everything they got. There were no allowances, no fancy cars, no expensive clothes. He wanted them to do something productive with their lives and not take success for granted.

Forrest Jr. and John Mars took over the company from their father and maintained the same ideology. The brothers and their sister, Jacqueline, shared a back office and one secretary. There weren't any executive perks or lavish company retreats. The family grew wealthy but never lost sight of its thrifty ways.

Today, the Mars company website still talks about the same principles. The family's story shows the importance of developing a rock-solid philosophy and living by it. Future generations will benefit. Best practices can be learned and passed on.

As an advisor to wealthy families, a former college admission dean, and a mother and wife who's also the primary breadwinner, I've seen all sides of families and money. We all need a better way for them to live in the same house.

Although most of us don't have a long term plan in mind when we start our families, it's precisely what we need to create a family that prospers beyond one generation. Those who truly understand wealth invest in their families with as much foresight as they do in their businesses. Family trips include activities that resemble those usually associated with corporate retreats, where workshops teach finance and philanthropy skills. From college admission tutoring to investing boot camps, no stone is left unturned when it comes to making sure the family's kids are positioned to succeed.

To organize your family with a business mind-set, here are my five principles to building a dedicated strategy.

Step 1: A Family on a Mission

A strong business begins with a well-thought-out mission explaining the purpose of the enterprise. A business with a written mission statement has double the return on equity as one that doesn't have such a statement. For families, the mission hinges on deeply rooted values as well as on a shared vision for the future.

Business leaders know that if they don't deliver on their promises, they'll lose their customers. A family that wanders off course runs the same risk with even greater consequences than lost profits. That's why starting with a clear mission is the first step for businesses and families alike.

For example, Cargill began as a modest grain storage facility on the American frontier in 1865 and has become the largest private company in the United States. Operating in 66 countries, it now provides food, agricultural, and industrial products around the globe and generates revenue rivaling that of Ford Motor Company. Cargill's vice-chairman described its strategy this way: "As far as how our corporate strategy works, we don't say, 'We think the world's going to look like this, so let's define our strategy for that world.' We don't know what the world's going to look like. We need a strategy or a set of strategies that can be successful almost irrespective of what the world looks like."[2]

This kind of forward-thinking philosophy is just as relevant for a family interested in long-term success as it is for a global, growing company. Neither can predict what opportunities and challenges will appear down the road. Cargill's mission remains firmly planted in its century-old founding vision. It's still successful today because its leaders recognize the company strategy has to evolve as times change. Families that strike a balance of staying rooted in their original principles while always planning for the future are also positioned for success. A written mission is the touchstone that connects the two.

Step 2: Values First

A healthy enterprise is defined by its values. These are the guiding standards that provide a compass for how people behave. This is true for employees in a business or members of a family.

If the standards are clear, the family will not only weather any storm, it will grow stronger. Smart businesses make sure their people make decisions with values up front. Families should do the same.

For Patagonia, the $600 million apparel brand, the corporate values are environmental consciousness. The founder, Yvon Choinard, started with this philosophy in the 1970s by making replaceable spikes for climbers, which caused less damage to rocks than permanent spikes. However, over time these spikes too were weakening the rocks, so Patagonia left the climbing hardware business altogether because it was out of sync with the company's strategy of being environmentally friendly. Patagonia started making clothing instead, and led the way with high-quality, green, recycled textiles and organic fabrics to become an industry front-runner.

Patagonia continues to live by its values. It is passionate about preserving nature and the beauty of the outdoors. In turn, it supports efforts to protect the environment. It puts 10 percent of its profits into environmental actions and is now one of the biggest B Corps, a designation that commits a company to make its business decisions based on environmental and community needs.

Families ought to make decisions this way too. For example, if a family believes that generosity is high on its list of values, the mission statement should say that members want to share their wealth. Then they should develop a strategy for giving to a cause they find important. If family members believe that being open and honest is important to the family's future success, then having a process that encourages good communication is essential. Some families believe in public service, so they mentor future generations toward careers in government or elected office. Other families are explorers at heart, and so they travel the world in search of new experiences.

Whether it's a sense of duty or a sense of adventure the family wishes to encourage, the key is to open up the dialogue to discuss the family's principles so that members remain connected as well as inspired. We wouldn't start something as simple as a family hike without a compass to stay on the right trail. Being clear about the family's values makes it easier to navigate the inevitable twists and turns on any family's path.

Step 3: Service with More Than a Smile

To last, a business has to provide benefits to its stakeholders. It's why customers buy from a company and why employees want to work for an organization. A family also has stakeholders, namely, its members. It provides benefits to them, both economic and emotional. Shareholders who get a return invest more and stay loyal. Family members will too.

A prime example of putting people first in business is SAS, a leading analytics software company. Its founders decided not to go public, which is unusual for a technology company that competes with big names such as Oracle and IBM. Instead, they invested in their employees by providing them with more benefits, including better medical plans, on-site day care and preschool, and other amenities. There were extra costs for these programs, but the savings in recruitment expenses paid for them. The company has one of the lowest employee turnover records in the industry. Happy employees are productive employees.

Like a successful business, a successful family is all about its people, who require support, training, and commitment to a purpose. They need mentoring to meet unexpected challenges. They need rewards to celebrate their successes. These are investments in the family's human capital that are more than paid for by ensuring the next generation's success.

For example, funding education increases future productivity by developing the skills and talents of the younger members. Providing emotional support and advice builds their confidence as they assume increasing responsibilities. Hosting frequent family gatherings creates strong relationships that keep the family connected. A family strategy requires input from all its stakeholders—its members—in order to be optimized.

Step 4: Plan the Work and Work the Plan

Laying out goals and objectives is standard operating procedure with any business plan. The same ought to be true for families. Whether financial or personal, wise families decide jointly what they want to accomplish then set about doing it as a team.

The southern supermarket chain Publix, the nation's seventh-largest private company, has thrived because of its decision to turn its 157,500 employees into stockholders. Publix is the largest employee-owned company in the United States, with 101,000 shareholders. Making employees owners encourages them to keep their customers happy, which has helped the chain achieve a higher profit margin than other public US supermarkets.[3]

Family objectives aren't always measured in dollars and cents, yet they are equally as important to a family's future. Whether it's fiscal strength or physical health, setting a goal keeps people focused. Some family members want to preserve the family history and some want to earn PhDs. Dividends without dreams don't last. Seeking wealth for its own sake ultimately proves to be a hollow ambition. It's what is accomplished with the money that provides lasting satisfaction. This means part of every family's strategy must include choosing the things that the family wants to focus on and working together to reach those goals.

Step 5: Strategize to Optimize

Good strategies are essential to achieving goals. Where should the energy be focused? How should resources be allocated? What are the barriers? Reaching family success is a campaign of the highest order, so it needs a plan, a staff, a timetable, and markers along the way. Whether at work or at home, it often takes a new approach to reach a lofty target.

No one thought that a coffee company could succeed in China. By aggressively changing its typical strategy when it entered the Chinese market, Starbucks has been going strong. Mindful of the Chinese tradition of involving the whole family in decision making, Starbucks invited parents to community meetings in Beijing and Shanghai. They were able to tell the company's story and why it's a great place to work. The company leaders were sensitive to the culture in which they worked and learned new ways to achieve the corporate goals.

Getting the older generation on board first allowed Starbucks to recruit a whole new group of brand ambassadors. This brought more potential customers and more potential employees because the younger family members were comfortable with Starbucks once they knew their elders supported the new concept. [4] Over 580 stores have already been opened in 48 cities, and 1,500 are planned by 2015.

Taking the time to understand a new market is paying real dividends for Starbucks. Engaging all its members in important endeavors is good for a family too. Each new generation brings a fresh perspective into the mix. Sometimes a different plan of action is warranted. Whether it's supporting a different social cause or selling granny's jewels, family decisions involve not only equity among the members but also emotions. Including everyone in the discussion early on pays off down the road.

*   *   *

Clients are often seeking financial advice, but frequently it's the family portfolio that we end up managing. Sometimes bad habits need to be corrected. Indulging kids with too much money not only hurts the finances of the current generation, it creates a sense of entitlement in the next generation. When couples put off financial discussions because they don't agree about financial goals, it creates more problems in the future. Even wealthy families have to make tough choices today to take care of tomorrow. That can be challenging yet necessary.

At home and in business, it takes courage to change course. A company can be slow to recognize that new products or services will soon make the current ones obsolete. Kodak, once known as a great innovator, failed because it wasn't willing to go digital. Even though one of Kodak's employees invented the first rudimentary digital camera well before the digital age, the leaders didn't recognize the potential. The company didn't want to risk losing money in its old standby, the film business. Clinging to short-term profits instead of investing in long-term gains is a hazardous strategy for a company or a family.

It can be tempting for families to cling to old ways too. Countless tales of fiction and fact are based on the perils of family honor, justice, and revenge. Businesses also run into plenty of disputes, but they're typically resolved, and people move on. Family feuds can last for years when someone doesn't inherit what they expected. It's best to have no surprises when it comes to money.

From Buffett and Gates to Bloomberg and Pickens, many of today's wealthy elite now say that they are giving more to charity and less to their children. Whether this strategy works depends not only on telling the kids they have to stand on their own two feet, but on having a plan that gets them ready to do that.

An Early Warning System

One of my shrewdest clients in business wasn't always so savvy at home. Ron's genius for turning new ideas into winning businesses was legendary. His tireless work ethic and salesmanship reaped him the financial rewards he'd always wanted for his family. When we met at our usual diner for a monthly breakfast meeting early one summer morning, the topic wasn't money talk. This time it was family talk.

A problem was brewing on the home front. His daughter, Catherine, was going through a rough patch. Her As and Bs in school had dropped to Cs and Ds. Her old friends weren't stopping by. The new ones were sullen and sly. It was a shock to the system in this hard-driving family where things usually ran according to plan. As a former college advisor, I'd seen this before.

"Janet and I are at our wit's end with Catherine. The more ultimatums we put down, the worse she gets. And her brothers are beginning to act out too," Ron said as we sipped our coffee.

"Has Catherine been tested for any learning or psychological issues?" I asked gently.

Ron was uncharacteristically quiet for a few minutes. "Well, we have to try something. How do we get this done?"

A detailed evaluation by a psychologist diagnosed a learning disability. Catherine was also depressed and anxious. She soon began intensive treatment, and together with Ron and Janet, we found a new school with a different academic approach. The girl responded well to the new environment. Her grades improved over the next year. The tension at home calmed down, and everyone's spirits rose again.

Although Ron was relieved that things had turned around for Catherine, this was a wake-up call for him too. In business, he had checks and balances to catch problems before they became serious. From factories to finances, he was alerted promptly if something was amiss. He didn't have the same systems set up at home. Many families have members who struggle to reach their potential. Being proactive about addressing problems contributes to a next generation that is healthy and productive.

A few months later, we met back at the diner for our regular catch-up. "I've been thinking more about my family since Catherine's troubles came to light. This kind of thing would never have happened at work. I'm always on top of problems there. The signs were there that Catherine was struggling, but we ignored them for too long. I guess we didn't want to admit that our family wasn't perfect. We need a better way to manage things."

Ron knew that businesses require constant attention. From cost cutting to employee morale to keeping meticulous records for every one of his ventures, he had handled all of the ups and downs of operating highly profitable companies. Every possible contingency plan was in place. But he didn't have a "manual" to help him run his family. It was running on autopilot.

I suggested we meet at his office next time. I wanted him to have his work hat on. As we got settled in his large conference room overlooking downtown Los Angeles, I gestured to a wall full of plaques. They had the names of his companies engraved on them along with their individual mission statements.

"Ron, what do you think is the key to your success in business?" I asked.

"When I start a new company, I always have a goal in mind. I have a vision for it. Then it takes good people, sound finances, and a lot of hard work to keep it going. Every time I do it, I'm driven to make it succeed." His voice literally boomed with these words.

"Okay, after you decide what the company is going to do and you have the right people hired, and some financial capital to get started, then what happens?"

"Well, we treat our customers well. If we make a mistake, we fix it right away. I take care of my employees too. I pay them well. We have good benefits. Loyalty is important."

"When you think of high standards, couldn't this be applied to your family as well?"

"Janet and I hope that our kids are picking up our values, but we've never really talked about it in so many words. We do worry sometimes about what will happen when we're gone." Ron glanced away, lost in thought.

"I notice you have your company values on your letterhead." I circled the words "Integrity, Service, Excellence," which were printed under his firm's name. "Have you ever thought about being that explicit about what they are for your family?"

Intrigued, he said, "I'd be interested in what my family members would have to say about all this."

"Ron, I suggest that we apply this same discipline to a strategy for your family. It starts by defining your family's purpose. Then we'll focus on the principles you and Janet want to pass on."

It was important that Ron be ready to engage the whole family in the plan, so I explained how the process works. "Your children are old enough to be a big part of this. From the family finances to the family trips, the idea is to decide together what your family wants to accomplish. Their opinions matter. You and Janet still call the shots, but what the kids think is important. It's not that different from those town hall meetings you have with your employees."

We worked together to develop a plan for developing the family's strategy. After the mission, values, and goals were agreed on, Ron and I met back at our old diner for our monthly get-together. He told me the conversations were starting to open up. The family dynamic was shifting slightly, but it was noticeable.

"Since we've started having meetings, our communication is so much better. We all use Post-it notes with our top three values printed on them. We talk more about our family budget. It's a time when we can talk about what's going on in each other's lives and how we can support one another more. We're getting on the same page. Finally." He raised his arms in a victory pose and smiled.

Thriving businesses and thriving families share a lot in common when it comes to their strategy. They both have a mission that inspires and energizes the members by keeping everybody focused on what matters. Taking care of the members keeps them productive and happy. Goals and objectives establish necessary milestones. Strategizing allows us to sculpt a future that doesn't just fit our family's needs but also helps fulfill our dreams.

* * *

Often we find ourselves riding along the highway of life, eyes fixed on the future, occasionally checking the rearview mirror, with money, success, and family security in our sights. Then suddenly we're caught off guard when something goes haywire. There'd been no warning light that we might be drifting away from values as we earn more and want more.

The right checks and balances keep things on track. Establish the ground rules ahead of time. Structure a sound support system. Solve problems early. Set worthy goals for the future. Keep learning. It's all part of a family strategy.

The ultrarich have always known that managing a family is part of managing money. In today's hyperconnected world, families cannot afford to think of their members and their money as mutually exclusive. From my own family to countless others, I've seen the same gap. There are plans for the immediate finances but no plans for the family. Getting everyone on the same page is what developing a family strategy is all about. Missions get crystallized. Goals become clear. As finances are fine-tuned, families get focused.

Jim Collins, the author of the best-selling business book *Good to Great*, was unequivocal on what it takes to make a good company great. He said: "That good is the enemy of great is not just a business problem. It is a human problem."[5] Money is made and lost every day in business, but the losses that are tougher to recover from are those that concern the family. Putting their strategy into action is how families can keep both their dollars and their sense.

CHAPTER 2

Mission: Keeping Your Family on Track

A company's mission is a clear and concise statement about its purpose. What does it aim to do? What value is provided? The business world has come to appreciate that customers listen to a compelling message. That's why companies spend so much on advertising and marketing. Scott Bedbury, brand guru for Starbucks and Nike, defines great brands as stories that are never completely told. A galvanizing mission is the first chapter of the story for a business or a family.

Before its legendary swoosh symbol, Nike's founders knew they wanted "to bring inspiration and innovation to every athlete in the world." This is their mission statement. To engage consumers in the story, they added a tag line: "If you have a body, you are an athlete." The appeal of contemporary brands such as Facebook and LinkedIn is that they connect people. Having a mission for your family creates its own social network.

Businesses big and small understand how missions move people. The Humane Society taps our emotions with its promise "to create a humane and sustainable world for all animals." Disney's aim is "To Make People Happy." The TED organization only needs the two words—"Spread Ideas"—to engage us in its cause. When a mission strikes a chord, everyone wants to be a part of the story.

Today's entrepreneurs plan meticulously to craft compelling missions for their companies, but tell them their family needs a mission, and you'll be met with blank stares. Though we now have more MBAs than ever before, it's the family balance sheet that remains misunderstood. An unfocused company will lose customers as well as profits. If family members don't understand what they are trying to accomplish, they are bound to get off track.

The first line on the website of the Coca-Cola Company drives home the point. It says, "Our roadmap starts with our mission." The roadmap for a family works the same way.

In successful organizations, employees have a clear grasp of what the company is trying to accomplish. The stock boy may not own company stock, but he certainly understands why he's there. Family members shouldn't function in a vacuum either.

A mission begins with a founder's vision. A founder is someone with the drive and ambition to create something of lasting value, such as a family or a company. If a founder built a company, the founder's family most likely understands what the business itself is all about. Mission statements are more commonplace there.

Even in families that have a family business family members don't always stay involved in it. Passing on the founder's vision for the family through a mission statement provides continuity for succeeding generations. Having a written statement helps them remember it. Remembering it makes it important.

The old proverb "shirtsleeves to shirtsleeves in three generations" relates to the challenge of successfully transitioning wealth past the second generation. It predicts that the money will be gone by the third generation. When that time comes, family members may have never met the family's founders. Perhaps they didn't hear the poignant personal stories of the challenges that were overcome. More than likely they didn't have the matriarch or patriarch as a mentor. They may have the trust fund, but money alone doesn't create the ties that bind.

This is when families need a mission statement. It instills the family's most important message in the minds of the succeeding generations. This can be expressed in a single sentence such as this one suggested by the six Smith family grandchildren when they gathered to talk about their family: "The mission of the Smith Family is to keep our family connected, be grateful for our good fortune, and share it with others."

We aren't accustomed to seeing mission statements in a family setting. They are often found in schools, places with a different job to do but like a family in important ways. Both are there to remind the next generation that others before them had a vision and acted on it.

Making Good on a Promise

For most kids, the first time they see a mission at work is at school. Those who are lucky enough to have motivated teachers and visionary leaders are taught that the whole is greater than the sum of the parts. Schools that instruct students about their missions as passionately as they do their academics transform the lives of their students. There is more than one kind of lesson to be learned.

Oil City Elementary is in a town of 3,000 people in northern Louisiana. Over 70 percent of the kids qualify for free lunches because they live in poverty. Some are homeless. Their challenges are many. When they get to school, they focus on their mission because they know what it is. They see it the first day on a plaque in the front hall, and they're reminded of it every time they enter the door.

"The Oil City Magnet School will provide an educational environment for all students to achieve academic success." Next to this message are three "rules of the road" that everyone lives by: "Be respectful. Be responsible. Be ready to learn."

Though these are simple words to write, the work is not easy to do. It happens at this school because the teachers and the administration have bought into the organization's purpose. It doesn't take a corporate logo and big marketing budget to create a great mission. It takes commitment.

Walk the halls of Oil City Magnet School and it's obvious that something good is happening. There's an intangible yet unmistakable positive vibe. Step into a classroom, and it's clear that teachers and students are rowing in the same direction. Everyone is on task. The task is learning.

The science lab is right outside. It's the woods the students call their playground. Students learn where water comes from and how to conserve it. There isn't a Whole Foods Market for miles, but there's plenty of organic lettuce. The kids grow it in their own garden. They also built a greenhouse and paid for it by caring for people's plants. They've bought into the plan.

The sound of opera wafts from the kindergarten classroom after lunch as the youngest kids rest. Meanwhile, the computer lab buzzes with activity. There's no graffiti on the walls. There are no chains on the doors. A wholesome environment is what the mission promises, and that's what's being delivered at Oil City Magnet School.

This can-do attitude isn't the norm in this nearly forgotten town. The difference is that these teachers and students have a mission that inspires them.

Instead of letting tight budgets or bureaucracy bury new ideas, every one pitches in to find a way to get things done.

Oil City's strategy is working. Kids aren't zoned out or constantly texting. They're tuned in to math and English. Test scores are among the highest in the state. Teacher turnover is low. Discipline problems are way down. Enrollment is way up. Success in this tiny, out-of-the-way town's school isn't about money. It's about mission.

Setting out on a mission should be an inspiring adventure. The dream should feel big. Think what it took for the Apollo team to put man on the moon. Most of us don't fly into outer space, but aren't we all reaching for the stars with our families? It begins with one person's dream. Soon it becomes a family's mission. Then it turns into an ongoing story in which all of the family members are the heroes.

A family's mission is more personal than a company's. It often takes root as a daily maxim. It might be a slogan or byword that rings true to someone. It's something to turn to when times get tough. A family mission gives purpose to its members' lives just like a company's mission provides focus to its employees. It's more than a statement on the wall. It's a way of life.

When a new company is founded, someone has to step up first with a big idea. The same thing happens when families start out. Bold missions can take hold quickly. Take Google, for example. Two Stanford University students started out by inventing a search engine for the school's computer system. Though their first office in a Menlo Park garage was modest, their ambitions quickly grew to mammoth proportions.

Google organizes information for the world. The company's products are used so universally that Google's website has become integral to our daily life. The company's employee-friendly workplaces are the envy of many with their perks. So are their jobs. A story that began with the dreams of two young men has changed the way the world lives and works. While there are many reasons for their phenomenal success, it wouldn't have happened without a mission.

Big Heart, Big Mission

Bird, Boa, and Sabo were the nicknames of Duane's childhood buddies. Everyone's economic standing was about the same in the rural plantation community on Hawaii's Hamakua Coast where he grew up. The little town has all but disappeared, but its impact continues. Duane takes it wherever he goes.

The family's financial resources were limited. Duane didn't inherit any assets or business connections when he graduated from the University of Hawaii. This bothered him at first, but soon he realized he owned something much more valuable. He had the power of his own story. He designed his mission around it.

When Duane moved to Honolulu for college, he did so on his own, paying for his education by working two part-time jobs. Today Duane operates a whole cadre of businesses. His companies run the gamut from media and technology to sports and food. But there's more behind this empire than merely the kinds of products and services the companies sell. All this business activity is rooted in the mission that grew from Duane's community. He puts it like this: "At AIO, we are dedicated to living and promoting the unique values of Hawaii, its culture, and its people."

For Duane this mission is universal. His companies aim to produce the best products and services in the world, but it's not the products themselves that make the difference. At work and at home, it's all about leaving the world a better place for future generations. That doesn't happen without family.

From the beginning, Duane's principles have shaped his mission. He first learned the importance of trust, respect, humility, and honesty from his small-town environment. These values have shaped not only his own family, but also his whole family of companies.

Two nonprofit organizations coexist with his for-profit organizations. They are all integrated in ambition and scope with what they do as a company and what they do as individuals. They serve their local Hawaii communities. They also extend their reach to Japan, a link to Duane's and his wife Susan's family heritage. The organization was the first on the ground with aid to the town of Sendai after the tsunami in 2011. Company and community go hand in hand.

Duane's mission of service is alive and well inside the company too. He sends employees as volunteers to villages in third-world countries to help build infrastructure, which helps the employees fulfill their own missions. Any employee can take an extra week off each year to spend time on a personal project or interest. It's not about professional development. It's about self-development.

I first met Duane when I happened to be seated next to him at a charity dinner. We struck up a conversation quickly because his interest in others is so intense that time isn't wasted on small talk. It didn't take long to find common ground.

I shared with him my belief that preserving wealth was about more than managing finances well. We talked about the importance of getting families to pass on their values, share their principles, and define their missions.

Duane read about corporate missions in business school, but he learned about the true importance of having one from his own family. With strong core values guiding him, Duane was motivated to succeed. He built his business philosophy around a mission to serve others, even while making money. He does both very well. His mission was clear.

Your family can plant similar seeds. It's hard to know in advance which ones will blossom. Tending to your mission keeps them growing.

As with any new project, a set of instructions can help you get started. These steps use a business tactic with a family twist to create a family mission.

Step 1: Send Out the Invites

When a company defines its mission, lots of people get involved. It isn't only the C-suite employees who set the direction. A special meeting is called to invite others into the mix.

Do the same with your family. If meetings aren't yet part of the family lexicon, this is the chance to start. Busy employees can always find an hour a week for a staff meeting. You can ask the same of your family. Choose a time and place and make it stick. Tell your family about the new project. Let them know this is a way for everyone to participate in how the family runs. To get started, everyone will complete a survey, such as the one at the end of this chapter, about the family. You'll discuss it at the next meeting.

Step 2: Ask for Input

We all like to be asked for our opinions, especially regarding matters we care about a lot. These days anyone with a smart phone is accustomed to completing a survey. Pick a few questions from my survey to customize yours. The questions cover a variety of topics, such as culture and values, the family's decision-making process, family business ownership, and philanthropy. You'll find the survey at the end of this chapter (pp. 30).

Once everyone agrees on the questions to ask, send out the survey and set a deadline for responses. Remember, your goal here is to find out what is important to your family members so you can create a mission that is meaningful to everyone. Consider having an objective person outside the family to keep track of the answers and compile them in a way that is neutral. A simple survey tool can help to organize the responses on a home computer. For smaller families this is fairly simple; for larger families with multiple generations this will be a bit more complex, but worth the time and energy. Then schedule a follow-up family meeting.

Step 3: Share the Results

The survey should begin with questions about values. Each family member chooses seven personal values, seven that best describe the family as a whole, and seven that are important for the future. Don't be surprised when there's a gap between where you are now and where you'd like to be. That's to be expected.

Families are filled with stories, but rarely is there a collection of them in one place. The survey helps to draw out the special memories and experiences that make up the family's true DNA. Questions such as the two that follow encourage family members to reflect on the things they cherish, the genuine family jewels.

"Please share an important family story or tradition you want preserved and handed down to future generations in order to help strengthen the family, preserve the family legacy, and understand the family's philosophy."

"What attribute or characteristic of your family do you value most and hope never changes?"

Step 4: Brainstorm the Big Ideas

Talking about the survey results is like holding a family focus group. Companies don't just guess how their customers feel about their products and services. They bring prospective consumers together for in-depth discussions. Families can generate the same type of valuable data.

A wise CEO knows the company's mission needs to keep employees connected to the company. This is no different at home. Shared values and shared stories lead to a shared mission.

At the end of the day, the mission should address the biggest family question there is: What does it mean to be us?

Step 5: Get Down to Business

A mission is a mantra that motivates. It's a motto to keep everyone in step. One family expressed its belief that everyone in the family is expected to make the family a priority with three simple words: "No Empty Chairs."[1]

Your mission is your family's promise to itself.

Step 6: Use It or Lose It

Learning takes practice. If you see something often enough, pretty soon it seeps in and becomes second nature. Put your family's mission on the refrigerator. Print it on Post-it notes. Practice it during your workouts. Then it will be top of mind when you need it.

Whether it's at work or at home, we're all faced with tough decisions. Making good ones requires not only knowing what to do but why we're doing it. There's not always time to ponder the big questions before every judgment. Mastering your mission means it will be there when challenges come along.

A family's mission is the first chapter of its story. The rest is like an epic tale filled with themes of new opportunities and learning unfolding with each new generation. Each person lives his or her own version.

Sometimes the plot gets complicated. If people have to read between the lines to discover the central theme, it's no wonder they start writing their own scripts.

Timeless Words of Wisdom

Whether you're a family of one or one hundred, what matters is developing the appropriate mind-set. We live in an era of unparalleled opportunities. To make the most of them, your family needs a strong philosophy. A mission statement helps you live by it.

The MacDonnell family linked its mission to its land. In the early 1980s, founders Bob and Jan bought the first parcel of what would one day become Round Pond Estate. Bob was engaged in a busy finance career, and the couple fell in love with the Napa Valley. They were drawn to the beauty of this rich, fertile part of the Rutherford region as a place to restore and retreat. They saw not only the potential to produce world-class wines and specialty foods there but a way to keep their family connected.

Bob and Jan's four children enjoyed special times at Round Pond. They played in the vineyards and learned the values of respect and appreciation for the land from their parents. As Bob's business career wound down, and the time came to plan for the future, Round Pond was a natural place for the family to focus their energies.

It had become the center of family life, and they described their philosophy this way: "Working the land, especially a great piece of land, is not about bending it to your will. For more than a quarter century, our family has strived to help this magnificent property evolve and achieve its full potential."[2]

For the MacDonnells, this philosophy applies to family too. Bob and Jan recognized that that their children needed the opportunity to continue the family legacy while forging their own paths. The second generation is now managing Round Pond's orchards and vineyards, and the family continues to nurture their land as well as their home.

The two generations have established a family council to govern the interests of the family and the business. They have a written agreement with a mission at its core: "The family council is created to help to ensure our long-term business and family success and prosperity."

The family council's mission is to articulate and preserve the family and business vision, values, and philosophy. The council holds family meetings to discuss business strategy and family strategy. Information and education are always on the agenda and so is fun. Though the third generation is still very young, its members will be in the mix soon. This family knows that strong family relationships and business success go hand in hand.

Involving the next generation in the family strategy is just as important to successful wealth transition as any investment strategy. That requires having a next generation with a mission in mind.

My firm invests money, so we think a lot about risk. It's what our clients hire us to worry about. How much will we earn? What's the chance of a loss? There's never a shortage of hazards to consider when it comes to the financial world. Everyone wants that crystal ball.

We can't predict the stock market. And the future's always unclear. But there is one sure thing: if you don't know where you're going, it's likely you won't get there. And that's a risk that's not worth taking.

Where's your mission taking you?

* * *

Sample Family Survey

Thank you for taking the time and for giving thoughtful consideration to these questions. Getting a clearer understanding of your family's culture and dynamics will help to build and foster a culture that sustains your family legacy and contributes to your long-term success.

The following questions explore your values, vision, philosophy, and your perceptions of what makes your family unique. These questions usually take between 30 and 45 minutes to complete.

Identify the range that captures the year you were born. This will help to understand the different perceptions and goals of the various generations in your family.

- Born between 1900–1930
- Born between 1931–1945
- Born between 1946–1965
- Born between 1966–1985
- Born between 1986–2005
- Prefer not to choose

Section 1: Culture

1) Please select the seven words that best describe your own personal values – the *values that motivate your actions as an individual and guide your decision making every day.*

- Admiration / Respect
- Ambitious / Motivation / Drive / Achievement / Accomplishment / Passion
- Artistry / Creativity / Beauty
- Athleticism / Fitness
- Autocratic / Dominance
- Awareness / Perceptiveness
- Balance (work/life)
- Care / Compassion / Empathy / Kindness
- Close-knit / Cohesiveness
- Confidence / Security
- Communication / Openness
- Competition

- Conservatism / Tradition / Conformity
- Decisiveness / Purposefulness
- Demanding
- Dependability / Trustworthiness / Loyalty
- Discipline
- Diversity
- Eco-friendly / Green (environment)
- Emotional
- Entrepreneurialism
- Equality / Egalitarian
- Excellence
- Extroversion / Camaraderie / Friendliness
- Family-oriented / Pride in family
- Forgiving
- Fun / Humor / Playfulness
- Generosity / Philanthropy / Charity / Altruism
- Gratitude
- Harmony / Agreeableness / Peace
- Health
- Honest / Candid
- Humble / Modest
- Inclusive / Belonging / Welcoming
- Independent / Self-reliant
- Individualistic / Distinctive
- Innovative / Ground-breaking
- Integrity / Ethical / Principled
- Intellectually curious / Smart / Intelligent
- Interactive (as a family) / Collaborative / Team-oriented
- Leadership / Control
- Legacy / Continuity
- Leisure-oriented / Laid-back / Relaxed / Carefree
- Logical / Sensible
- Materialistic / Spender
- Open-minded
- Patient / Long-term
- Perfectionist / Meticulous

- Persistent / Stubborn
- Political
- Positive / Happy
- Practical / Realistic
- Private
- Prominent / Desire Recognition
- Proud
- Proper / Formal
- Responsible / Reliable / Consistent
- Risk-taker
- Satisfied / Content
- Socially Conscious
- Spiritual / Religious
- Spontaneous
- Status-conscious / Celebrity-conscious
- Stewardship
- Successful
- Thoughtful / Introspective
- Thrifty / Prudent / Frugal
- Traveler / Adventurous
- Worried / Nervous

2) If you could add one word or phrase to the list of values to further describe your personal values, what would that word or phrase be?

3) Please choose <u>seven</u> values that you think represent the *collective* values of your family members as you know them today.
- Admiration / Respect
- Ambitious / Motivated / Driven / Hard-working / Goal-oriented / Passionate
- Artistic / Creative / Cultural
- Athletic / Active
- Autocratic / Domineering
- Aware / Perceptive
- Balanced (work/life)

- Caring / Compassionate / Empathetic / Kind
- Close-knit / Cohesive
- Confident / Secure
- Communicative / Open
- Competitive
- Conservative / Traditional
- Decisive / Purposeful
- Demanding
- Dependable / Trustworthy / Loyal
- Disciplined / Structured
- Diverse / Valuing Diversity
- Eco-friendly / Green (environment)
- Emotional
- Entrepreneurial
- Equality / Egalitarian
- Excellence
- Extroverted / Talkative / Social / Friendly
- Family-oriented / Pride in family
- Forgiving
- Fun-loving / Humorous
- Generous / Philanthropic / Charitable
- Grateful
- Harmonious / Agreeable
- Healthy / Health-conscious
- Honest / Candid
- Humble / Modest
- Inclusive / Belonging / Welcoming
- Independent / Self-reliant
- Individualistic / Distinctive
- Innovative / Groundbreaking
- Integrity / Ethical / Principled
- Intellectually curious / Smart / Intelligent
- Interactive (as a family) / Collaborative / Team-oriented
- Leadership / Control
- Legacy / Continuity
- Leisure-oriented / Laid-back / Relaxed / Carefree

- Logical / Sensible
- Materialistic / Spender
- Open-minded
- Patient / Long-term
- Perfectionist / Meticulous
- Persistent / Stubborn
- Political
- Positive / Happy
- Practical / Realistic
- Private
- Prominent / Desire Recognition
- Proud
- Proper / Formal
- Responsible / Reliable / Consistent
- Risk-taker
- Satisfied / Content
- Socially Conscious
- Spiritual / Religious
- Spontaneous
- Status-conscious / Celebrity-conscious
- Stewardship
- Successful
- Thoughtful / Introspective
- Thrifty / Prudent / Frugal
- Traveler / Adventurous
- Worried / Nervous

4) If you could add one word or phrase to the list of values to further describe your family's *collective* values, what would that word or phrase be?

5) Please select seven values or attributes that you believe are critical for the future long-term success and happiness of your family. Note that these aspirational values for your overall family may or may not be the same as the values you chose in question 3.

- Admiration / Respect
- Ambitious / Motivated / Driven / Hard-working / Goal-oriented / Passionate
- Artistic / Creative / Cultural
- Athletic / Active
- Autocratic / Domineering
- Aware / Perceptive
- Balanced (work/life)
- Caring / Compassionate / Empathetic / Kind
- Close-knit / Cohesive
- Confident / Secure
- Communicative / Open
- Competitive
- Conservative / Traditional
- Decisive / Purposeful
- Demanding
- Dependable / Trustworthy / Loyal
- Disciplined / Structured
- Diverse / Valuing Diversity
- Eco-friendly / Green (environment)
- Emotional
- Entrepreneurial
- Equality / Egalitarian
- Excellence
- Extroverted / Talkative / Social / Friendly
- Family-oriented / Pride in family
- Forgiving
- Fun-loving / Humorous
- Generous / Philanthropic / Charitable
- Grateful
- Harmonious / Agreeable
- Healthy / Health-conscious
- Honest / Candid
- Humble / Modest
- Inclusive / Belonging / Welcoming
- Independent / Self-reliant

- Individualistic / Distinctive
- Innovative / Ground-breaking
- Integrity / Ethical / Principled
- Intellectually curious / Smart / Intelligent
- Interactive (as a family) / Collaborative / Team-oriented
- Leadership / Control
- Legacy / Continuity
- Leisure-oriented / Laid-back / Relaxed / Carefree
- Logical / Sensible
- Materialistic / Spender
- Open-minded
- Patient / Long-term
- Perfectionist / Meticulous
- Persistent / Stubborn
- Political
- Positive / Happy
- Practical / Realistic
- Private
- Prominent / Desire Recognition
- Proud
- Proper / Formal
- Responsible / Reliable / Consistent
- Risk-taker
- Satisfied / Content
- Socially Conscious
- Spiritual / Religious
- Spontaneous
- Status-conscious / Celebrity-conscious
- Stewardship
- Successful
- Thoughtful / Introspective
- Thrifty / Prudent / Frugal
- Traveler / Adventurous
- Worried / Nervous

6) If you could add one word or phrase to the list of values to further describe your aspirational values for your family, what would that word or phrase be?

7) What attribute or characteristic of your family do you value most and hope never changes?

8) Is there any topic or issue that you wish your family would discuss, but does not?

9) At age 95, what would have been most important to you in life?

10) How would you describe your family's collective goals, fundamental purpose, and/or philosophy? If you're not sure, please answer "not sure."

11) Please share an important family story or tradition you want preserved and handed down to future generations in order to:
    a. Help strengthen the family
    b. Preserve the family legacy
    c. Understand the family philosophy

12) Please use the space below to share your personal resume. This is an opportunity to describe those interests and passions that drive your thoughts and motivations.

13) Do you have any final thoughts you would like to share that elaborate on answers you provided or help us know your family better?

Section 2: Decision Making

14) How would you describe how decisions are made by your extended family?

- Family leader decides
- Family leader decides with input from a small circle of family members
- Majority rules
- Consensus among all adult family members
- Other – please describe

15) I believe family decisions should be made based on input from all adult members of the family.
- Strongly Agree
- Agree
- Neutral
- Disagree
- Strongly Disagree
- No Opinion

16) I feel free to express my ideas and opinions to my family.
- Strongly Agree
- Agree
- Neutral
- Disagree
- Strongly Disagree
- No Opinion

Section 3: Stewardship

17) I would be willing to work together as a family to articulate and clarify our values, our family's culture, and how our family's "uniqueness" drives our family governance process going forward.
- Strongly Agree
- Agree
- Neutral
- Disagree
- Strongly Disagree
- No Opinion

18) I believe I have the knowledge and experience necessary to assume responsibility as one of the "stewards" of my family's wealth.
  • Strongly Agree
  • Agree
  • Neutral
  • Disagree
  • Strongly Disagree
  • No Opinion

Section 4: Family Business

19) I feel ownership in the family business strengthens my identification and connection with the other family members and family overall.
  • Strongly Agree
  • Agree
  • Neutral
  • Disagree
  • Strongly Disagree
  • No Opinion

20) If I remain an owner in the family business, one of the reasons is that I believe my investment will provide me with a better financial return than if I sold my shares and invested the money elsewhere.
  • Strongly Agree
  • Agree
  • Neutral
  • Disagree
  • Strongly Disagree
  • No Opinion

21) I believe the family should establish a process allowing family members to sell shares for "fair" value and remain engaged with the family in other ways.
  • Strongly Agree
  • Agree
  • Neutral

- Disagree
- Strongly Disagree

Section 5: Philanthropy

22) How would you define philanthropy?

23) Do you think it's important for your family to be involved in philanthropy? Why or why not?

24) Engaging in philanthropy as a family is a way for us to establish common values and to foster the continuation of those values for successive generations.
   - Strongly Agree
   - Agree
   - Neutral
   - Disagree
   - Strongly Disagree

25) I am interested in learning about the passions and interests of my family members and in sharing my own.
   - Strongly Agree
   - Agree
   - Neutral
   - Disagree
   - Strongly Disagree

26) I believe that the philanthropic interests of all family members are equally important and should be all taken into account in deciding how to distribute grants between organizations.
   - Strongly Agree
   - Agree
   - Neutral
   - Disagree
   - Strongly Disagree

If you chose D or E, please explain below:

27) In making charitable contributions, do you want to help solve immediate social problems, invest in long-term change, or both?

28) As you make philanthropic investments, do you want to support established organizations, new products, or both? Why?

29) Are you currently interested in a cause, movement, problem, or question?
    a. What is it?
    b. In your opinion, where is the most help needed (research, humanitarian aid, political activism, etc.)?

30) Would you feel comfortable sharing this interest with your family? Is this a cause that you hope your family might consider donating to?

31) Do you want your family's charitable gifts to support a wide range of projects or focus on just one, or very few?

32) Do you want to support local, national or global projects?

CHAPTER 3

Vision and Values: Put Family Members and Principles First

S trong values are the backbone of a good business as well as a good family. Whether protecting a corporation's brand or a family's reputation, values are key. Much as a firm can be damaged by fraud, a family will suffer if it puts its money ahead of members or ideals. Taking shortcuts never pays.

Today's companies put their values up front. Whole Foods Markets built its whole business on a commitment to healthy eating. With its tagline of "A Family Company," Johnson & Johnson lived by its values when it ordered an unprecedented $100 million recall of Tylenol following reports of cyanide poisoning in 1982. Strategies should be flexible but ethics shouldn't be. As much as families talk about values, we rarely see those set down in writing. Most of us have some vague sense of a "family code." What we need is a way to make values a real asset a family can built on. That is, the values need to be defined and communicated.

Though a company's mission rarely changes, a dynamic, ever-adapting vision is necessary for a company to stay current. In 2009, the tough economy hit Starbucks hard, and the company's performance faltered. Sales went down. The stock price did too.

Stores were closed, and people were laid off. The company's leader realized it was straying from its core vision of creating a distinctive culture and experience for its customers. Customers returned because they realized they were getting more than just a cup of coffee. With the right leadership, a company can turn itself around. Starbuck's edge came back along with its profits.

The bottom line for a family is more than financial. It's personal. Whether in business or at home, success is driven by the leaders' vision and values. The leaders set goals and inspire through their actions. Smart companies make sure their decisions are guided by their principles. Smart families do the same by making sure everyone knows what the family's principles are. Then it takes good leadership to help the family live by those principles.

Call for the "All Hands" Meeting

The role of chief executive officers is to stand at the proverbial helm and guide the ship. They are hired for their vision. They're expected to practice what they preach when it comes to principles. So when a successful, respected chief executive contacted me about his family, he was unaccustomed to being at a loss for solutions. He was beloved by his employees as a decisive leader who took good care of his people. His corporate strategy was going according to plan. Things weren't so good on the family side.

"I've worked hard to do everything right," he told me when we initially talked on the phone. "I don't need more wealth management. I need family management."

The first time I met with Jack and his wife Laura, they welcomed me into a grand and gracious home. We gathered in a wood-paneled den lined with family photographs from their world travels. At first, it was like sitting down as old friends, and they were both cheerful and chatted amiably. But as soon as I turned the conversation to the topic of their family, concern showed in their eyes as they described the disengagement of the members.

Over the past year, Jack and Laura's three adult children had become distant from their parents and from each other. One had started a new job as a litigator with a demanding trial schedule. Another was beginning a new career as a corporate executive, a lifestyle that required frequent international travel. Another was starting graduate school and was busy with her studies. Everyone was polite with each other; yet, they didn't seem as close as they once had been. Gradually, attendance at the formal Sunday dinners at Jack and Laura's home had waned.

"Things have gotten offtrack," Jack said in a serious tone. "Our kids just don't seem to be that connected any more. Everyone is in their own silo."

"We seem to be losing touch with what we always said our family was about," Laura added with worry in her voice.

"What would you do in your company if your team became disengaged?" I asked.

"That's easy," Jack said. "I'd hold a corporate retreat with our key people. We'd go back to remind ourselves of what made us successful in the first place. We'd get back to basics. Get everyone on the same page."

"Good!" I said. "Let's do the same thing with your family. We'll start with a survey to get everyone involved."

"I know my family," Jack insisted. "I don't think we will learn anything new from a survey."

Though this seasoned professional was well aware that a "top down" approach was outdated in the business world, he wasn't thinking that way on the home front. I wanted him to consider the possibility that his family members might have different goals for the family now than they did when they were younger. That didn't necessarily mean there was a problem with values. It might be a communication gap.

These days we as consumers are asked to evaluate virtually everything. We rate the products we buy, the hotels we visit, our fellow employees, and our country's leaders. But we rarely have the chance to reflect on how our families are working.

Business leaders appreciate that corporate culture can make or break a company. My approach with families is based on the same principle. Every family has a unique culture. It's made up of the attitudes and values of the members. We assume we understand what makes our family tick. However, when we stop to ask, we're often surprised.

Jack and Laura remained skeptical, so I described how the survey worked. This would be a time for family members to express their *own* views about the family. As adults, their children have new and varied interests that are important to each of them. Sometimes family dynamics get stuck in the same old stereotypes and habits. Members lose interest if the family isn't growing along with them.

"The kids are already so busy with their jobs," his wife said, worried. "Between school and activities, the grandkids are consumed with their own lives. Even if they filled out the survey, would everyone be honest?"

Jack wore a worried expression. "I always thought this family would be set by now. I expected our children to be successful and happily married and that our extended family would be really close. But we just keep drifting further apart."

"Just because our lifestyle worked for us doesn't mean it was going to be right for them," Laura told Jack. "We focused on the finances but neglected to ask everyone what they had in mind for themselves. Now they are adults with their own problems to solve. Maybe it's time we started talking."

This was a conversation I'd heard before from other family leaders. They had a vision for their finances, but as time passed they sensed that the family was not as connected as it used to be. The first step was to send a letter to everyone to introduce the family survey. Answers would be anonymous, and we'd share the results at a family meeting held at a favorite resort at the end of the summer when schedules were more flexible. I collected all the email addresses, sent off the first communication, and set a two-week deadline.

Responses poured in quickly via the user-friendly online survey. The answers were genuine, emotional, and surprisingly candid. Each participant chose the qualities that best described the family, including attributes, aspirational goals, favorite stories, and personal interests. The replies made it clear that family values hadn't changed; they were merely out of focus.

When I meet with families, I ask members to describe their mission and to define their values. Most of the time, the response is a blank expression. Values aren't clear because they've never been discussed. Typically, the leaders get so focused on *what* they are doing that they forget to talk about *why* they're doing it. My survey encourages family members to think about their family in a new way. They consider what should never change and what should be open for change. Some principles are renewed. Others are amended.

Evaluations are standard procedure for planning and problem solving in business. A family evaluation accomplishes the same objectives. It's a time when everyone who is part of the enterprise has the opportunity to assess how things are working, to recommend improvements, and to recommit to the family's future.

The morning that I'd been invited to join Jack, Laura and their children Mike, Dave, and Ann for their first formal meeting, the atmosphere was one of quiet anticipation. As we began to discuss the survey results together, everyone was surprised at learning so much about each other. The son Mike, who was a litigator, suggested changing the family gatherings. His schedule just didn't allow for long Sunday dinners every week. He said he wanted more from the family than a "check the box" contact. Dave, a corporate executive, proposed a weekend retreat, planned far in advance so that everyone could be there. Maybe the family could include outside speakers. He wanted to talk about ideas.

Ann wished her Dad could be less controlling. Jack wanted time with the grandkids. Laura wanted everyone to get along. In other words, these were typical family dynamics.

Despite the disparities in personal needs, all family members agreed that they wanted to work together to strengthen their connection and communication. They all signed a family agreement that defined their values and stated their mission. "The mission of the Thompson Family is to achieve growth and prosperity, both as a family and as individuals. We value family pride, the entrepreneurial spirit, and individual responsibility."

This was the beginning of the Thompson family members' renewed commitment to each other. Their regular family meetings evolved and expanded, with the goal of fostering connections and communication among the siblings and the cousins.

Years later, the group continues to gather for its annual meeting. Now the meeting place is selected not by Jack alone, but by a "retreat committee" of family members. A discussion about investments with the family's financial advisor keeps everyone in the loop regarding money. Jack and Laura have shared information about their estate plans, including a letter to everyone describing their hopes and dreams. They always had a vision for the family, and now everyone shares it. These meetings are family reunions but also so much more! Honest communication is where opportunity starts, and future checkups are required for the family to stay healthy.

*   *   *

Research shows that visionary companies have outperformed the stock market by a factor of 12 since 1925. In their book *Built to Last: Successful Habits of Visionary Companies,* authors Jim Collins and Jerry Porras define a "visionary company" as one that is a premier institution in its industry, is widely admired by knowledgeable businesspeople, has made an imprint on the world, has had multiple generations of CEOs, and has multiple product or service life cycles.[1] Businesses like Walgreens, Abbot, and Nucor have met these tests of time. Companies that can keep alive the passion and innovation of their founders beat the odds. The same can be true for families.

Achieving continuity from one generation to the next requires a similar blend of inspiring vision and openness to fresh ideas. Creativity and innovation aren't only important in business. They are the ingredients that keep families growing and thriving.

Opportunity Lost

Facing change takes courage. A family that built a grocery store chain brought me in when tensions were rising. I met with the owner of the chain and his two sons in the company warehouse office. A photo of their immigrant grandparents hung on the wall, a reminder that sacrifice and hard work could lead to good fortune.

The grocery business had healthy finances, but family members bickered and sniped at each other at every opportunity. Eager to stop the infighting, the father of the family and his sons agreed to launch the survey with more than thirty members across four generations. Once I'd gone over everyone's responses, I could see that they were still in sync on their common values. Loyalty, responsibility, humility, and family pride were repeated over and over again in the survey. Values were intact.

When I delved deeper into the surveys, I saw a few cracks appear in the foundation. Many family members were concerned about how decisions were being made. Most felt more input should be sought from the whole family. Only a handful of family members said there was enough communication. More than a few didn't feel comfortable expressing their own ideas or opinions at all. Seeds of discontent had taken root because some family members felt communication was stifled. They needed to open up the dialogue.

When I presented the results to the family, everyone seemed on board and ready to take steps to address the concerns. I went to work with the sons on a plan. We developed ideas to expand communication and drafted a protocol for making family decisions. In the weeks that followed, though, attention waned. Eventually one of the sons told me they'd decided not to pursue the process any further.

Profits in the grocery business may not have dropped that quarter, but a crucial opportunity for progress in the family was surely lost.

*   *   *

Everyone expects there to be ebb and flow in business. However, applying the credo to "never give up" to our families can be more difficult. Decisions about how to take care of the family don't seem as clear-cut as decisions on how to run a business. Anyone who understands how to make money knows that it takes hard work and perseverance. If we apply the same zeal to our families, our investment returns will be high.

Values together with the attitudes of the employees guide the way a business operates. Much as a firm can be damaged by taking shortcuts, a family will suffer if it puts money ahead of its members. For both a business brand and a family's reputation, adhering to values is key, especially so when leadership changes.

The Next Generation Steps Up

One Thanksgiving weekend I met with five siblings whose parents had passed away in the course of the past year. We gathered in the family home at the kitchen table, boxes filled with china and other mementos stacked around the room. The house had been sold, and the estate was being wrapped up. It was time to move on.

Or was it?

The family attorney introduced me to each of the adult children. He described the family's background and explained that the parents had been frugal; through wise investments and careful planning they had saved much more than their modest lifestyle showed. Each of the children would be inheriting a sizable nest egg. They sat quietly during the attorney's explanation of how the assets would be shared among them. The family business would continue to operate, and they would become the new owners. As they realized all their parents had accomplished, the siblings started to reminisce.

The eldest son, whose hair was gray at the temples, broke the awkward silence. "I had no idea Mom and Dad saved so much."

"They were thrifty," the youngest daughter said, fighting back emotion. "They never spent money on anything except the business or us."

"They really worked hard. That's all they did," added the middle son in a respectful tone. "Dad never called himself an entrepreneur, but now that I'm one myself, I know it was his example that inspired me."

The younger son offered a faint smile. "Think about the dinners we had at this very table. Remember the biscuits Mom made every Thanksgiving? Who has that recipe anyway?"

"I don't know if she ever wrote that down, but there's a lot more we don't know," the oldest daughter replied wistfully. "It was hard to get Mom and Dad to discuss their feelings. I wish we had asked them more questions about what they thought about things. Everyone was always too busy."

"This happens often in families," the family attorney offered sympathetically. "But since the five of you are going to be in business together in the future, this is the perfect opportunity to think about where you'd like to go from here."

"Mom and Dad always treated others well. They didn't talk about the good things they were doing. They just did them," added the youngest daughter.

As an advisor, I've seen this time and time again. When the parents pass on, their children feel a sudden disconnect. The family is left with questions. It's a fragile time. Being clear on values unites the family members.

"Even if you've lost the family recipes, you haven't lost the family spirit," I told them. "Now it's your turn to make sure you find a way to carry that forward."

"Maybe we can do that in our own way with some of the money," suggested the oldest son. "It seems like we should do something to honor them. What if we gave a gift to charity?"

"Mom and Dad left us all the ingredients," the middle son said. "We just need to mix them in our own way."

With the help of their advisors, this second generation set up a private foundation and launched their family philanthropy efforts. Working on charitable projects helped the siblings focus on what they have in common and led them to work together in a way they never had while their parents were still alive. They defined the causes they wanted to emphasize for their giving. They agreed on roles and responsibilities. This new endeavor gave them a path to the family's future even as they mourned their loss.

This family was fortunate to have good relationships in place when the founders passed away. Even with that head start, the new leaders still needed to learn how to communicate and make decisions together. Philanthropy gave them a way to do that and also helped them articulate the family's values.

* * *

It's no secret that successful families should take care of their financial assets. They don't want to lose their money. But what about the loss that occurs when families don't preserve their hopes, dreams, and values? Do they understand what is really important to them or the true purpose of the family?

Whether in a great company or a great family, core values drive the big decisions. For example, from day one, Southwest Airlines' founder let it be known that the company was committed to the customer experience.

Likewise, for Volvo, brand identity is synonymous with safety first. Top-performing companies build values into their strategies because today's consumers want to support businesses that impact society for the better.

Window-dressing statements won't cut it anymore. Consumers now seek out companies that "walk the talk." Values generate revenue more than ever before. The next time you pay your credit card bill online, click on "Blue Box Values" of American Express and you'll see "integrity," "teamwork," "respect," and "accountability" highlighted on the website. You would want to see these same things in your own home. When leaders tackle the crucial task of inspiring this way, everyone wins.

But sometimes businesses can lose their way. Families can lose their trust. When this happens, hard work is necessary to right the wrongs, and this doesn't often happen overnight.

This was the case for a young woman who came to see me, concerned about how she and her brothers could work with their parents to transition the family and business leadership. The restaurants they owned weren't doing well. The parents were tiring of the long days, and the operations needed tightening. Finances and feelings needed mending after a quarrel over who would run the business. She knew the status quo wasn't good enough for the future of the business or the future of the family.

After we discussed using a survey to plan for a family meeting, she was enthusiastic. We would ask for input about the important decisions facing the family. "This is a great way to unite everybody. I'll talk to my brothers about getting started."

Then nothing happened. After several months, she called again. "I just can't get everyone to agree to a family meeting. They say they like things the way they are."

This young woman had hit a roadblock in her family. She was open to change and saw how it could benefit her family as well as its business, but she was the only one with that insight. Progress would have to wait.

* * *

Breaking new ground is hard. Even Steve Jobs couldn't convince Apple of his new ideas in the early days. Industrial innovation requires time, money, and dedication. It's a massive commitment. Changing minds and opinions is equally difficult in a family, if not more so.

In a business as at home, keeping vision and values intact and practicing them is a challenge, especially when problems arise or personal tragedy strikes. For families, this is about more than recovering a year's profits.

A Family Reclaims Its Legacy

A crossroads can be an opportunity to either prosper or falter. When the leaders of a respected family came to see me, they were at just such a junction. After 150 years and a storied history, the current generation was considering how to plan for the future and wanted a formal process to help make the necessary decisions.

One of the questions on the family survey provided the answer. The question we asked was: "Share an important family story you want preserved and handed down to future generations."

Some fascinating words appeared on one of the surveys: "Farming, mercantile, real estate, education, oil, and gas." While this looked like a list of business holdings, a powerful family story lay just beneath the surface. The family members wanted to ensure that the family's history was handed down to future generations, but so far the story hadn't really been told yet.

Back in 1880 when the first generation began farming in the rural South, cotton was the crop of the day. Over two decades, the family steadily acquired more land and became the largest cotton grower in the state. The family members purchased paddle wheelers to get the cotton downriver to the markets and bought ten mercantile stores along the route so their returning boats could bring back other goods to sell in their shops.

But soon floods, boll weevils, and the financial panic of 1907 devastated the business. Farms were sold. Times were rough. The family made paying off all their debts a top priority and maintained good relationships with the bankers. Later on, when family members decided to start all over in a new venture, their bankers were happy to help.

The only land they could afford this time was in a backwater underdeveloped area, but family members approached an area college about relocating the campus to their town. The family gave the school a piece of the land and helped raise funds for the new buildings. This made the remaining land more valuable and also launched a young college into its second century of educating the region's most promising young people. A member of the family has sat on the board of this college ever since. The current patriarch served as the chairman of the board during the 2009 financial crisis and led the school through those tumultuous times.

Soon enough this new location brought an opportunity to invest in the early pipelines for natural gas. In addition to building a new livelihood for the family, the pipelines supplied the first gas street lights to the community. The current gas utility still operates under this first charter.

In spite of smart choices, challenges kept coming. Heartbreaking illness and accidents claimed precious lives and required new leaders to step up. The family oil and gas business eventually blossomed. Along the way the family made a commitment to community philanthropy. Today the family office still has one of the "family coins" made of copper—the currency of the time—as a token of the triumphs and sacrifices along the way. It was copied and distributed to today's family members as a way of preserving the family legacy.

The heirs knew their family history well. It wasn't a distant story. It was a cherished memory. It was their identity.

When I read each member's personal comments on the surveys about how they continually check plans and adjust strategies to stay flexible, I saw a family whose vision and values were in lockstep. Giving back was deeply embedded in their DNA, as was clear beyond any doubt from the comments family members had sent. We designed the family's first formal meeting to discuss future goals.

The family members decided to keep working together in business and in philanthropy, not out of habit, but because of their renewed commitment to the family's vision and values. They could not have done this without a process where they could hear each other and find an attachment to their shared roots.

Companies run on numbers. Families run on values. Good business sense is about more than getting a small return on your money. It's about generations of returns.

Money can either unite or divide us. The money doesn't decide. We do.

Getting Your Family on Board

CHAPTER 4

Forging Family Partnerships

Doing business today is all about teamwork. The era of the lonely lighthouse keeper is a thing of the past, as are the command-and-control CEOs, dispensing orders from their own kind of tower. These days, workers have to collaborate to get the job *and* get the job done. Family members are just as interdependent. Call it being connected to common ground.

It's not just the old team stereotypes that don't apply anymore. Whether it's managing global supply chains or responding to increased shareholder scrutiny, companies across the board are realizing that bringing the collective intelligence of the firm into the mix means better decisions. Families can also use their own internal smarts to their advantage by making sure that members work together effectively.

The results of all this sharing speak for themselves. Businesses that outperform their peers are 30 percent more likely to identify openness as a key influence on their results.[1] These company leaders recognize that collaboration works. When asked who they want to hire in the future, they describe people who can thrive in the company's team-based environment. There's no place for the words "I just didn't feel heard" on the feedback form anymore.

This is good news for families. The track record of family businesses points to the opportunities a family environment offers to foster effective teamwork. A study at Texas A&M University revealed that family-owned operations beat other firms in revenue and employment growth and have a longer-term view of investment. They're more stable, and they inspire more trust as well as commitment in their employees.[2] Families are hardwired to do this well, but they also need to work at it.

A family and a company's workers have something in common when they start out. They're each brought together by a combination of fate and a shared purpose. Ultimately, for each of them, their biggest challenge turns out to be the same. It's a matter of how to turn raw talent into a real team. Technology can get members connected, but it takes strong communication to achieve shared goals.

Trust is what ties everything together.

In large corporations as well as small family businesses, building effective teams takes concerted effort. Families shouldn't expect their teams to form and develop on their own any more than companies do. Whether in businesses or in families, financial resources alone can't guarantee success. It's how people work together that drives them forward.

Get People Talking

Pixar is the hugely successful movie studio that created the *Toy Story* hits and is renowned for employees that produce second-to-none creations. "Taking one for the team" wouldn't be the assumed default option in a culture like this. However, at Pixar that's what happens.

Pixar is so passionate about excellence that three years into the work on *Toy Story 2,* the company ditched the whole thing and started over. Pixar simply had to get it right. That movie became a blockbuster. So what made this movie studio such a powerhouse?

Many people give the credit to the late Steve Jobs, who invested in the company and later ran it. Though he was revered for his genius at design, for all of his computer savvy, Jobs believed that it wasn't more technology that would make Pixar shine. It was teamwork.

Jobs insisted that the physical layout of Pixar's office make face-to-face interaction a necessity. He pushed for a central space where people would be forced to run into one another. Whether you wanted to go to a meeting room or a bathroom, you bumped into coworkers at every turn. People didn't rely on instant messaging to share an idea or debate a solution. They talked in person. Communication clicked. They would settle for nothing less than the stellar results their best team effort could bring.

Companies still ponder what it takes to create that magic synergy. You know it when you see it, yet it seems hard to engineer in advance. Families thrive when they have that special sauce at work too, because good communication is the key to good relationships. Most of us don't have a genius like Jobs in our midst. But we can apply a little scientific method in our own homes to get the team fires burning.

In business, holding in-person meetings is standard procedure. Dr. Albert Mehrabian's research indicates that meetings are more effective than the written word or telephone conferences because 55 percent of the meaning and feeling of the communication is carried in facial expression and nonverbal signals.[3] For problem solving, brainstorming, and building trust, there's no substitute for getting the group together in person to keep everyone in sync.

The same holds true in families. According to the research of expert family business consultants Craig E. Aronoff and John L. Ward, family meetings are the best way to help family members discover and build on common ground that unites them.[4]

However, there's more to having good meetings than just getting the group to the conference table. MIT researcher Alex Pentland studies how teams work. In his research, participants wear electronic sensors that measure an individual's behavior in a group. It turns out that voice tone, hand and arm movement, and the frequency of speaking compared to listening are critical to the team's overall success. The results boil down to four points:[5]

- To be effective, a team requires maximum communication between members during meetings. A dozen or more interchanges between people during every meeting is ideal.
- Everyone must participate. No one person should dominate.
- Members of the team should keep talking informally, and often, outside of the regular meetings. Casual conversations build collegiality.
- The team should also brainstorm with others and bring new ideas to the table for discussion to encourage dynamism.

A surprising note about this research is that these factors had more impact than skills and smarts combined. Although the study was conducted with business in mind, it applies equally to families. Talking is not enough; families need teamwork too.

Good family teamwork keeps the lines of communication open. The more engaged members are as group, the more effective they are in maintaining the family's shared purpose. Working together toward common goals inspires commitment.

Here's a translation of the above tips for the family context:

- *Treat your family like a team.* Schedule formal meetings and send an agenda that includes topics of interest to everyone. Face-to-face is best, so plan well ahead and consider timing and locations that will best meet everyone's schedule while at the same time setting the expectation that the meetings are a family priority. Keep the family's mission and values at the top of everyone's mind by reviewing them at the beginning of every meeting.
- *Share the podium.* Rotate the job of leading the meeting among family members. Mom or dad shouldn't always run the show. Encourage everyone to speak up. Listen to different points of view. No interrupting.
- *Practice.* Look for opportunities to talk to one another frequently between formal meetings. These days we have to be reminded to unplug if we want to connect with family members. Texting and email can be a cop-out at home, just as they are at work.
- *Brainstorm with others.* Consider inviting advisors or experts to attend the meeting to educate family members on specific topics, such as finance and investing, estate planning, or philanthropy. Other outside speakers can be chosen in accordance with the family's mission and values or based on specific interests of family members.

Aronoff and Ward also found that by participating in regular meetings together, bonds were created that sustained the family even during challenging times. Spending time on teamwork early on is an investment in the family's future.

Greg and Judy Roberts's story provides a good example. When Greg's health began to fail, his family had already been holding regular family meetings for several years because the family members shared ownership in various investments. By the time they had to face a different kind of issue, they were already an experienced team.

We've Got Your Back, Mom

"I need some help," Judy said tearfully to her kids when we got to the part of the family meeting reserved for sharing and open discussion. "Greg isn't doing well. He's forgetting things. His headaches are worse, but he doesn't want to talk about it. I can't get him to see his doctor. I'm sure he's afraid of what we'll learn."

Everyone had seen the signs that led to Greg's Alzheimer's diagnosis. But he was so good at forging ahead that it was easy to be in denial. Judy still thought of him as the hard-driving executive who never missed a beat. He made decisions a mile a minute, never leaving a detail undone. But things were changing fast. All in the family were fooling themselves by hoping his health would get better. It wasn't going to.

Several years earlier, before there had been any signs of health issues on the horizon, Greg and Judy had met with their attorney to do some estate planning. He encouraged them to discuss their financial affairs with their children, who were all adults quite capable of running the numbers. Given the significant resources the children would be inheriting, the attorney wanted Greg and Judy to take their planning a step further and engage the entire family.

My phone rang the next day. The attorney told me their story. We set a meeting with Greg and Judy, who were openly curious about what more there was to be offered.

"What's left to do?" questioned Greg, almost as soon as we sat down at their big round table in the kitchen. On the walls were photos of the family on trips that crisscrossed the globe. There were shots of them on safari with elephants, hiking in the Galapagos, skiing in the Alps, and surfing the waves off the Maui coast. This was a family of people who welcomed adventure wherever they could find it.

"Once we're gone, the kids will each get their share of the money, and that will be that. They can do whatever they want then. It's up to them."

"Yes, you could leave things that way, Greg," I agreed. This wasn't a guy one could sell easily. He had to come to his own decisions. "But what if you could see your family in 100 years, still together, growing even stronger, carrying on what you and Judy started. Wouldn't that be worth a little more talking now?"

"I'm not sure we're going to change anyone at this stage," said Greg, doubt in his voice.

"Think about it from a business perspective," I told him. "Why do you have a management team? Why do you have staff meetings? What are the people around you there for?"

"My job is to think about the big picture. There's the money side, the product side, the customers. I have a great team that works well together. We've built a solid company culture. It pays off in profits."

Judy smiled and nudged him, catching on.

"Greg, your family is the same. Put your kids to work for the home front. Give them a chance to step up to new responsibilities. You already have the makings of an amazing management team. Imagine your great-grandchildren seeing the same sights that are in all these photos some day."

"Everybody's busy, but if we can find a time, let's give it a try," Greg agreed. The family set aside half a day over a summer weekend for the first formal meeting.

We discussed the kinds of things the family could do to strengthen ties among members, beginning with regular family meetings including Greg, Judy, and their three adult children. All five liked the idea of formalizing their roles as family leaders by establishing a family council. The two generations would discuss, deliberate, and make decisions about matters important to the family. They had a number of joint investments and were considering expanding those. They wanted to educate the grandchildren about the family heritage and build close bonds. They also wanted to have fun. By starting when the group was small, they could establish traditions as well as trust in working together as a team.

The Roberts family council decided to meet twice a year. The family members prepared for their first meeting by completing my survey, which helped them to define their collective values. Greg and Judy recognized that it was time their adult children knew more about the wealth they would inherit one day, so they began by reviewing finances, investments, and estate planning. They understood that providing information and education would give the next generation the skills they needed to be good stewards and guide the family's future.

A family council can talk about more than money. The Roberts family liked to debate ideas. From geology to archaeology, the family used these meetings to nourish members' intellectual side. There was only one rule: everyone had to be prepared and everyone had to participate. In addition to including educational topics, each meeting was followed by a special dinner with spouses and grandkids as well as the taking of a commemorative family photograph.

Learning and love were always on the family's agenda.

Meetings of the Roberts Family Council

Year One – Agenda for First Meeting

Icebreaker   15 minutes

Some families find it helpful to start with a warm-up activity to help every-one to relax before beginning the formal meeting. This can be especially useful when the family is just beginning to hold family meetings. One idea is "Picture Your Legacy," a set of image cards that guides families toward articulating their legacy.[6] Family members choose their favorite cards and tell each other why they made that choice.

Discuss the Results of the Family Survey   1 hour
    Approve Mission and Membership of Family Council
        "The purpose of the Roberts Family Council is to strengthen the family, support its members, and preserve the family's wealth."
    Ratify Core Values
        Honor, Fairness, Kindness, Truth

Review Issues Suggested for Future Meetings   15 minutes
    Family Wealth
        What assets do we own? What is the money for?
    Family Health and Harmony
        How do we improve our physical and spiritual health?
    Education and Training of Family Members
        How can we teach the grandkids about money?
    Intellectual Enrichment
        What new ideas and topics do we want to learn about as a family?
    Family Fun
        Annual family trips: Where do we want to go?

Choose Focus Topic for Next Meeting   10 minutes
    Family wealth: review of family investments

Family Speaker   15 minutes
    G-1 shares its wishes for G-2 (can read a letter or speak informally)

Open Discussion   20 minutes
    Comments from family members

Wrap-Up   15 minutes
    Agree on date, location, and focus topic for next meeting

Year One – Agenda for Second Meeting

Icebreaker

> *G-1 shares a story and photographs of early family ancestors*

Review Mission and Values

> *Honor, Fairness, Kindness, Truth*

Focus Topic

> *Presentation on family finances and investments (financial advisor as guest)*

Family Speaker

> *G-2 member proposes an itinerary for a family adventure trip*

Family Open Discussion

> *Family agrees on trip location and dates for trip to include the whole family*

Wrap-Up

> *Family decides to review estate plans as the next focus topic*

Year Two – First Meeting

Icebreaker

> *G-2 members congratulate parents on anniversary with gag gifts*

Review Mission and Values

> *Honor, Fairness, Kindness, Truth*

Focus Topic

> *Review of estate planning strategy (attorney as guest speaker)*

Family Speaker

> *Mom talks about her 50th college reunion and what education means to her*

Open Discussion

> *Family members decided to make a charitable gift to mom's college to honor her*

Wrap-Up

> *Family selects physical health and nutrition as next focus topic*

Year Two – Second Meeting

Icebreaker

> *Student speaker from mom's college who received the family scholarship*

Review Mission and Values
> *Honor, Fairness, Kindness, Truth*

Focus Topic
> *Family health and harmony: Speaker on nutrition and exercise*

Family Speaker
> *G-2 member shares her health challenges*

Open Discussion
> *Family members respond with support and encouragement*

Wrap-Up
> *Family selects philanthropy as next focus topic*

Year Three – First Meeting

Icebreaker
> *Grandkids surprise visit with photos from family trip*

Mission and Values
> *Honor, Fairness, Kindness, Truth*

Focus Topic
> *Philanthropy advisor speaks on family charitable giving as a teaching tool*

Family Speaker
> *G-1 member talks about the importance of being grateful*

Open Discussion
> *Family members share thanks*

Wrap-Up
> *Family selects intellectual enrichment as next topic and invites local author as next focus topic speaker*

* * *

By the third year, this family team had hit its stride.

Then Greg's health began to fail.

He missed the last meeting. No one knew he wasn't coming, but he just didn't show up. That's when Judy asked for help.

The kids didn't hesitate. They went into crisis response mode, offering sympathy, strategies, and support. After some brainstorming, everyone had a job to do to. Someone arranged for household help to relieve Judy. Calendars were synchronized. Doctors were called. The family had already been in training. Now the team was called into action.

As Greg's health declined, the family council met more frequently to oversee the business interests that had been on Greg's plate. A medical expert was called in to educate the family on how the disease might progress. The emotional strain was painful; yet the family was using its resources to solve as many problems as it could.

Setting up the family council early on had made it easier for the family to deal with important decisions when they arose. Being informed about the joint finances in advance paved the way to make better decisions later. The learning curve wasn't so steep, even for those not very skilled in reading balance sheets. Instead of spending time thinking about what they might inherit one day, family members spent the time being all they could be.

After Greg passed away, I heard from Susan, one of his daughters. "We're still having our family meetings. That time together really helps us stay on the same page. We're sad, but we're also strong."

*   *   *

The more experience a family has working together, the better it will get. If the first time the family has a meeting is to discuss who's going to inherit the family vacation home, don't be surprised when things get tense. Running a family is the ultimate team sport and takes practice.

It also takes planning. Once the family works in a more businesslike fashion, more business is bound to follow. With a mission statement in hand, values in mind, and a regular meeting date on the calendar, the way the family works soon becomes a little more formal. This is predictable, and it's progress.

Meetings give everyone a chance to weigh in on what's important. With a family, there's always something going on that could use input from the entire group. Someone is bound to need a sounding board. Just asking for opinions keeps everyone linked in.

Family meetings build trust and teamwork. This is a forum to share information and learn in the way that fits a family's unique personality. For families just starting out with formal meetings, a shorter agenda may be more productive. At this stage, the objective is to become comfortable with a group discussion by the family and about the family. The idea is to make it easy to develop the habit of having family meetings.

Family members should also look to these meetings as a source of personal encouragement. At each meeting some families include an open discussion to give members a chance to talk about something they are working on, a recent accomplishment, or a problem they'd like to brainstorm. Other family members then have the opportunity to offer support to the family speaker or to add suggestions from their own experience.

Over time, family members become more comfortable participating in the discussions. The subjects and the time frame can evolve and expand. Then the team will be ready when it's needed most. The best emergency plans are prepared way in advance.

In business, leaders know that they have to plan for the future. The founders know they won't be there forever. Like every good business team, a great family team will rise to the occasion.

It just needs to learn how.

Family unity doesn't happen simply because people share the same address. Having a sense of belonging is what matters. For example, Pixar's experience reminds us that a certain amount of face time matters. Family meetings make this time meaningful as well as fun. Whether you take your family thousands of miles away or take a walk around the neighborhood, staying connected is the key. It's not always convenient, but it's always crucial.

Owning a business can give a family something tangible to work on together. Much has been written about the opportunities and challenges those families face. However, every financially successful family has a lot at stake, whether the family name is on a business or not. Whenever there's a family, there's a partnership. It can be dissolved through disagreement or disinterest. Or it can develop into a dynamic force for progress. Members have to want to make the partnership work.

Families offer vast untapped potential, but it is easy to postpone pulling everyone together to make the most of this potential. Pressures of daily duties pile up. People get sidetracked in their own worlds. Investing in building a family team is as important as investing in the family finances. One really can't succeed without the other.

Keeping your family ties intact takes teamwork. Once these good habits are formed, they will pay good dividends for years to come.

CHAPTER 5

Setting Goals and Celebrating Milestones

If our mission gives us purpose, our goals help us fulfill our mission. The legendary radio announcer and motivational speaker Earl Nightingale placed responsibility squarely on our shoulders when he said, "We become what we think about."[1] Deciding exactly what we want to accomplish is the first step.

From the accomplishments of ancient explorers to the inventions of modern entrepreneurs, ordinary people have always been able to achieve extraordinary things if they set goals. Magellan went around the globe. Microsoft put computers on every desk. A company improves lives by selling a new product or service. A family improves lives by motivating its members to succeed. A family's specific goals define exactly what that means.

Whether it's getting in shape or getting a college degree, we all have things we want to do to improve our lives. Too often the resolutions made on New Year's Day are nowhere to be found by the time our summer vacations roll around. From our firms to our families, it takes drive and determination to get tasks off the to-do list.

For example, Henry Ford wanted to produce a low-cost car. He knew the world would be changed if automobiles were within reach of average Americans. With that objective in mind, he built a company to get the job done. We can do the same in our families by being clear about our aims. A family working together can be as powerful as any Fortune 500 company. The difference is that our strength need not be measured by how much money we make, but by what we do with it.

Dreams of Distant Lands Come True

Today travel is easy via online reservations, but for travelers in the nineteenth century, getting from one place to another was a challenge, if not a hardship. In the early 1800s, most people still traveled by horse and carriage. It was only in the late nineteenth century that railways changed people's habits. Even then, people in remote areas still relied on horses. Then along came traveling preacher Thomas Cook, who had a strong sense of wanderlust. He realized that others were interested in going places too, so he struck a deal with a new railway company to receive a share of the ticket sales to accommodate his large group of religious devotees who wanted to attend what we might call an out-of-town convention. Thus, the first travel agency was formed.

Cook kept going with his travel theme. He set one new goal after another, expanding to international destinations and launching the traveler's check concept. His business life wasn't without its difficulties, but he persevered. He opened the possibility of travel to the general public, literally changing the lives of ordinary people.

Cook didn't allow the limitations of the day to diminish his dreams. He set out on a path and found a way to offer a new service to people. In pursuing his passion, he discovered his purpose. More than a century later, the name Thomas Cook Travel brings paradise to mind when we imagine the excitement of visiting faraway lands. Though the business he founded has evolved through the years, Cook's mission had staying power because he tied his goals to achieving a good outcome. While he made a profit from his business, what lasted was his idea.

It's easy to misunderstand the purpose of our money. It's not destined to exist merely as a separate stash socked away in a secret vault. For wealth to grow, it has to become a part of our psyche. It's a stimulus for change. That change can be for the better or for the worse. It all depends on our goals.

Without the right targets, a company will go under. Whether it's bringing a new product to market or getting new customers, there has to be a driving force to get the firm to the next level. While a company's earnings or a family's wealth are tangible outcomes, those who succeed over the long haul have goals that aren't measured only in financial terms.

Going for results at any cost is a slippery slope. One only needs to look at corporate deals gone bad to be reminded that fame and fortune can be fair-weather friends. The Enron blowup and the Madoff money scandal are high-profile cases where greed got the best of people. Bad behavior can bring down any business or any family. If the objective is to get ahead no matter what, the decision is bound to backfire.

Prestige, power, and privilege can be seductive. It's smart to have financial aspirations, but the ends don't always justify the means. Good health, sound relationships, and personal fulfillment are equally important to a family's happiness. After all, success is a balancing act that requires constant attention.

One size doesn't fit all when it comes to people and their desires. What motivates one employee sends another's numbers down. The same is true for the members of any family.

For example, kids today feel intense pressure to measure up. Expectations can be especially high in affluent families. Whether it's on the soccer field or on the SAT, kids seem to face a tense race to the finish line from day one. Providing the next generation with the education and skills needed for the future is a worthy goal. This is about supporting them with formative experiences, not waging a competition for the most popular brand as a ticket to the top. The college admission process is a rite of passage for the family and often is viewed as a measure of success. It's important to remember that finding the best match might not always mean choosing the biggest name.

The College Sweepstakes

It was a crisp fall day on an idyllic college campus. Professors and students strode purposefully to and from their classes. The old hall, dating back to the college's founding in the 1800s, was filled with dozens of high-school seniors and their parents who were making the rounds through the New England countryside during the annual pilgrimage known as the "college visit."

At the time, I was the dean of admissions of one of the most selective liberal arts colleges in the country. With only a few hundred spots available to each entering class, the competition was fierce. I met with hundreds of aspiring applicants each year. Many of them were the sons and daughters of alumni who hoped that such prized family connections could give their children the edge they needed to get the sought-after admission nod.

One morning, from the front reception room of the white farmhouse that was home to the Admission Office, I saw a young man pull out a navy blazer from the trunk of his car. He and an older man of unmistakable resemblance straightened their ties one last time. The two of them, father and son, opened the wide, creaky door of the 200-year-old building where thousands of teens entered each year for their interviews with an admission representative.

Minutes later, I greeted the pair and explained the interview protocol. I would spend some time alone with the young man, then meet with the two of them together. As I learned more about the candidate's academic background, high-school performance, and test scores, I knew it was going to be a tough case. His highly competitive high school sounded like a pressure cooker, and his grades showed that he was feeling it.

"Tell me a little about yourself," I asked the young man as he fidgeted nervously in his chair.

" I'm looking forward to going to college. At my high school, everyone seems the same. They all want to go to Ivy League colleges and make a lot of money. I'm not interested in that," he said apologetically, looking down at his feet.

"Is there something that you've really enjoyed that you can tell me a little about?" I inquired, trying to draw him out.

"Oh, I spent last summer at this great place. It was a camp for kids who had problems. But I found out that they were really a lot like me. We all feel worried that we won't be able to make it in the world. They just needed a buddy. It felt good when they talked to me." His voice grew more confident.

"Have you ever thought about working with young people as a career?"

"My father and grandfather are both successful lawyers. They've always told me they want me to follow in their footsteps. But I'm not so sure that's for me. They are alums. They want me to be one, too."

"Yes, your family has a long tradition in this community. But what's your take on going to college?"

After a pause, the young man looked up, his eyes filled with tears, and said pleadingly, "I don't want to go here. Will you please tell my father that?"

"There are plenty of good colleges that would be great choices for you. Let's talk about some ideas, and we'll discuss it with your dad."

As we chatted a little more about his interests and came up with a list of other colleges for him to consider, the worry washed from his face. Then I asked his dad to join us.

"I've had a great conversation with Will today," I told his father, "and we have some ideas about college that he'd like to talk with you about. One thing that he shared with me is that he believes that there are some schools other than this college that would be better choices."

"But this is our family's school. It's what we've always planned on. I don't understand what you're getting at," his father stammered, agitated.

"Going to a good college is a great thing," I said calmly, trying to keep the dialogue open. "But sometimes keeping up a family tradition isn't the best goal for a young person when it comes to choosing the right school, career, or life path. I think Will is going to do just fine in college, but he wants to go in a new direction. My recommendation is to support him as he does that."

Will and his dad left my office and joined the other families on the campus tour. Several weeks later, I received a note from his father. He thanked me for the advice and said that after some soul-searching, he had backed off on pushing his alma mater. Will had applied to his first-choice school and been admitted. The son was on course and so was the family.

The college admission process was a defining time for this father and son. An expectation to continue the family tradition of attending a prestigious college almost short-circuited the young man's own goal-setting process. Fortunately, he had the courage to speak up. My role allowed me to be a sounding board. His father also needed advice even though what I told him was not the answer he wanted to hear.

*　*　*

There are times in a family's decision making when outside input is advisable. Especially for families of influence, it is useful to have someone who can ask the tough questions and who has no self-interest at stake. The life choices of the next generation make up one important area where family members can be working at cross-purposes.

There are others that bear watching closely.

For example, are the family's financial goals realistic? Are members as healthy and productive as they could be? Are any of the family's internal relationships in need of extra attention? Call it family therapy if you like. Sweeping problems under the rug just makes them bigger down the road. Facing a challenge before it becomes a full-blown crisis clears the path to achieving progress, no matter what the goal.

Even the best plans won't go anywhere without the right incentives in place. A good manager appreciates that sales won't soar without an appropriate bonus plan. Family members need incentives too and not only financial ones. Young employees are interested in career advancement. Young family members want to earn more freedom and responsibility as they grow older so that they are as prepared as possible for making their own decisions.

This can be a tough balancing act when it comes to families and money. If we give too much too soon, the rewards come so easily that there's no reason to work hard. If nothing is shared along the way, the kids aren't prepared to handle money and responsibilities later. Many an inheritance has been blown by bad decisions that could have been prevented with better preparation.

This is a time for the Goldilocks approach. Families that strike a balance are generous with resources that encourage productivity but also set limits on how much is available. A family bank isn't the same as a family wallet. The bank expects a return on its investment. The wallet merely runs empty. Cost of capital is an important concept to master, whether in a business or in a family.

The Carrot and the Stick

"Don't forget the sunscreen and the big pot for the gumbo," Frances called out to Jim as he loaded the family station wagon with the games, toys, and gear that signaled a weekend at the fish camp. The Bakers had rented a modest cottage on the Gulf Coast for the annual Labor Day festivities that marked the end of summer. Frances and Jim had enjoyed the more relaxed atmosphere away from Boston and the rigors of their academic schedules of teaching and research. Their four kids had finished their summer jobs at various camps and local establishments. Soon the school routine would resume, but this weekend was all about fun.

There was, however, one piece of important business on the agenda. That's why Frances and Jim had asked me to join them. Several months ago, Jim had called to discuss an exciting development, one that presented the family with new decisions. He and Frances had held onto the acres of land that he'd bought years ago when he thought he might return to his home state after graduate school. They never got around to building anything on it. So when the people from the oil and gas company wanted to lease it for drilling, he shrugged and said, "Why not?"

The signing rights for the drilling alone made them millionaires. This brought financial security that their academic careers never could have provided. Frances and Jim didn't change a thing about their lives. This was a one-time windfall, after all.

No new houses. No new cars. They invested the money and looked forward to a comfortable retirement. Enough said.

But then they hit pay dirt. The well came in, and it came in big. Frances and Jim were in new financial territory now. They would have wealth beyond their wildest dreams. But they were very clear about what they wanted to do. They also knew what they didn't want to do.

"We know the word is going to get around quickly," said Frances. "It's a small town. And even though we aren't around a lot, the kids are going to hear about the new oil well. Before they get any big ideas, we want to tell them about our plans."

"We've talked about this, and we plan to give most of this money away," Jim continued. "This is a poor community. There are so many people here who could use real help."

"Oh, we'll do things to help our kids, definitely. Just not *too* much," Frances went on to explain. "Education, maybe a down payment for a house, and a nest egg for each of them. But after that, we want them to make their own way."

We met Sunday morning in the comfortable screened porch. Frances and Jim described the family's unexpected good fortune, and what they would be doing. "You kids may hear our names associated with a big oil deal. It's true. We are a part of that. We'll be able to help you get a comfortable start in life, but we don't believe in retiring to easy street before you begin," Jim told them flatly.

The children's ages ranged from 11 to 17, just the ages where they could easily be swayed by money.

"Oh boy, can we get a fancy limousine?" asked Justin, the youngest.

"Forget about a car. What about a plane?" exclaimed the oldest brother, Brendan.

"Let's go on a cruise," suggested Sara.

"No, a trip to Hawaii," Jane shouted.

Jim and Frances settled everyone down and continued, "Our friend Linda is here to talk with us about a new project we are going to start. It's called a family foundation, and we're all going to be a part of it."

That summer weekend transpired over twenty years ago. Early on, the children weren't able to play active roles, but Frances and Jim always included them in discussions. As they grew up, so did their level of participation.

To date, the family's charitable gifts have totaled over $100 million since Jim and Frances received their first fortune. Their four kids went on to do just fine with their own goals and plans. They had no expectations of receiving great wealth from their parents.

It turns out there was more than one big well. Frances and Jim saw their wealth multiply many times over. As they watched their children's lives unfold, they were gratified that they had been able to provide their kids with resources for wise investments and ideas. Ultimately, everyone received far more than anyone could ever have expected.

Frances and Jim used the carrot and the stick. When the family's financial wherewithal changed, Jim and Frances took advantage of a teaching moment. They were generous with their newfound resources but not reckless. The family stuck to its goals at a time when it could have gone for a short-term payday. Prudence paid off many times over.

* * *

All work and no fun can cause bad morale in a company or a family. Celebrating milestones is important. If employees burn out, results suffer. From bonus plans and promotions, when a company rewards its employees, it also reaps rewards. A savvy family plan offers benefits too.

Sharing information is the first step. Whether it's the company's balance sheet or the family finances, we all like to know how things are going. The big decisions will come from management, but the whole team should understand what drives the numbers. When a destination is reached, everyone should be asked to join the party. Later, if belts need to be tightened, the troops can take that in stride.

Everyone also wants to know what to expect for their own advancement. In a company, it might be annual raises and a two-week vacation. Members of the next generation should understand what the family will provide them and what they need to do to earn it. A young associate works hard to make partner and usually knows how long that takes. In families, too, members need to know how to reach the next level, even if that level only means receiving the keys to the family van.

How to Mark Your Family Milestones

Step 1: Determine what you are striving for – *Establish a goal.*
- *Example: Achieve and maintain harmony within the family.*

Step 2: Assemble your support team – *Share your plans with your family, get members' feedback, and refine the plan.*

- *Founders and leaders tell the family that having good relationships with each other is an expectation.*
- *Reinforce values that support reaching the goal, such as kindness, compassion, and understanding, even when there are differences of opinion about a decision.*
- *Establish a written code of conduct for how family members treat one another.*

Step 3: Begin the work – *Call support team into action; provide frequent updates to make sure the plans are well structured; encourage and motivate.*

- *Hold regular family meetings to encourage open communication and problem solving.*
- *Treat children equitably with regard to financial rewards, such as gifts, loans, and inheritances.*
- *If there is a family business, set clear expectations regarding the roles of family members as employees and shareholders.*

Step 4: Reach the halfway mark – *Recognize your progress; take stock of the plans and refine as needed.*

- *Discuss estate plans and strategy with adult children to avoid surprises that can lead to conflict in the family.*
- *Call in outside experts if needed to resolve conflicts between generations, siblings, or cousins.*

Step 5: Congratulations! *Celebrate your success. Debrief and review the experience to pave the way for the next phase.*

- *Invite the extended family to a weekend retreat to celebrate an important milestone, such as a major family anniversary, family business event, or personal accomplishments of family members.*

* * *

Whether it's the company's retirement plan or the children's college fund, long-term investments generate more than income. They build loyalty. Good businesses always take care of their shareholders, whether it's a public company or a family-owned shop. Just consider the turnout to hear Warren

Buffett's wisdom at the annual Berkshire Hathaway meeting. Go the extra mile on education. It always pays off.

Being a part of a great company or a great family is a reward in itself. We just need to make sure our family members see it that way. From the company picnic to the family vacation, special gatherings are full of potential for all kinds of perks. Companies hold corporate retreats, complete with interesting speakers and entertainment. From taking group adventure trips to working on philanthropy projects, convening family members to learn something new together builds bonds of goodwill.

A company's marketing department is often in charge of its events. The family council is the ideal group to plan versions of such events for the family. Every group needs a social director, and it's likely that the perfect candidate for this role is already in your family. Asking everyone for input about the family's social events keeps all members involved.

Every office has a way to celebrate when something good happens on the team. Whether it's the ten-year pin or a party after a promotion, people like to know their efforts are appreciated. Families have plenty of things to celebrate. From birthdays and bar mitzvahs to promotions and paydays, everyone likes to be remembered. Giving kudos for reaching important personal goals is a must. It's the rare employee who doesn't like to be recognized in public for a job well done. The same is true for a family member who works hard to accomplish something. In your family, when someone graduates from college or climbs the highest peak, let the person know you noticed.

When family members are appreciated, they feel even better about being a part of the team. When they reach their goals, they gain confidence. They're likely to keep doing the right things. Success breeds success.

The word "congratulations" never goes out of style. Hearing it means you did something well. When your family reaches a milestone, give everyone a pat on the back. Take a deep breath and head for the next marker.

CHAPTER 6

Every Family Member Matters: Roles, Responsibilities, and Making Decisions

ounders always launch their new ventures with high aspirations and optimism regarding their success. Some are able to transform their vision into a way of life so it continues for generations, well beyond the time of their own personal involvement. In other cases, companies collapse during a crisis or fade away gradually for lack of leadership. This scenario occurs in families as often as it does in businesses.

Thomas J. Watson, an American industrialist who ran IBM for over four decades, developed the powerful sales culture that propelled his company's growth into a global force. The company not only survived him, it became a corporate giant. By contrast, Robert Maxwell's publishing conglomerate collapsed after his death. Even though he rose from poverty and put all of his energy into building his empire, the Maxwell companies applied for bankruptcy in 1992. One culture thrived while another one failed.

Building something of lasting value was of utmost importance to Ernest Butten, an entrepreneur who created a dramatically different outcome for Personnel Administration, the company he founded in 1943. Leaving nothing to chance, he set down his vision for the company shortly after founding it in a written document called the "PA Charter." This proved to be a pivotal step.

The PA Group grew to be one of the world's largest management consulting firms. When Butten retired in 1970, he produced a video in which he described the company's fundamental principles to new recruits. He not only had a vision, he also created a legacy by passing it on successfully to those who followed him.

Butten's example demonstrates the importance of making sure people don't function in a vacuum. From start-up to blue-chip company, business leaders put things in writing to clarify objectives and to keep the teams working together smoothly. Documents such as bylaws are a given in a large corporation, but even a small company has an operating agreement to set out how decisions will be made.

These days, when new partners start a firm, they understand that having a written contract just makes good business sense. If all the terms are agreed upon and defined in one place, there is less room for misinterpretation. A well-drafted agreement is the basis for building trust.

The earliest evidence of a written code dates back to 2300 BC, when a Sumerian king recognized the value in setting forth the rights of individuals and how they would be governed. Since then, governments and companies alike have been run according to formal agreements. Such agreements serve as the fundamental reference point for how things get done.

An agreement can be called a contract, a code, a charter, or a constitution. Name it what you like, for a business to prosper despite inevitable changes, it needs a framework to guide its progress. Families also benefit from having written guidelines to encourage a shared understanding of their philosophy and principles as they transition from one generation to the next.

Although written agreements for families are less common, there are some good examples from which we can learn. The 2002 American Family Business Survey found that 35 percent of business-owning families have a family agreement.[1] These families recognized that they have a great deal at stake and that having a stated agreement better preserves the family wealth, which is often closely tied to the success of the business.

In its publication "The Family Constitution Guide," the law firm Taylor Wessing defines a family agreement as "a written statement that serves as a record of the family's heritage, culture, hopes and ambitions for future success, as well as a plan for how to achieve them."[2] This is a tangible reminder of the family's vision.

The constitution articulates the family's mission and values. It guides the family's work as a team by describing the leadership structure that will manage the family's affairs. It supports the family's goals by establishing policies to lead it from one generation to the next. It's the guide to the family's future.

Any family that is committed to a long-term strategy would benefit from having a family agreement. If it has written down its mission and defined its values, the core tenets of its philosophy are in place. If it has begun to hold regular family meetings, it has demonstrated a commitment to work together as a group. If it has set goals for the family, it is planning its future purposefully. With these five steps in place, the family is ready to develop a written agreement:

1. Strategic outlook
2. Mission statement
3. Common values
4. Strong teamwork
5. Future goals

This is an opportune time to tie the family's work together through a document that sets out the rules of the road. Strong momentum and high engagement contribute to a process that everyone feels a part of. Family buy-in equals family success.

A Third Generation Looks Ahead

Roger's voice literally boomed with enthusiasm when he called to talk about his family. "We have an awesome family, and we're ready to do a family constitution," he announced with clear pride. This was a millennial leader proud of his family's past, but he was also eager to put his own stamp on the future.

"We own a great business that my grandfather started. Dad runs it now. We have the estate planning in place, the trusts and so on, and we've held some family meetings. We've been to seminars where we learned about family constitutions, but we need help figuring out exactly what to do and how to go about it," explained young Roger, a charismatic, committed young man in his thirties, who was now managing the family office.

This family now in its third generation had solid roots, and it was reaching an important time. They could plant deeper roots or let the future take its own course. The family members had good instincts and good intentions. Now they needed a plan.

Roger's grandfather, Peter, had emigrated from Europe in 1949 and founded the family business, a car dealership, in 1953 in southern California, east of Los Angeles in an area that was ripe for development in the 1950s. The company grew and prospered along with the region, and Peter remained CEO and president until his retirement in 2000. His son, Bill, runs the company today.

Bill and his wife, Beth, have raised three children who are committed to continuing the strong family values into the third generation. When young Roger called me, it was clear that many of the steps were already in place. Most important, the family was committed to working together to grow as a family enterprise. All members were ready to move forward, but they just didn't know quite how.

"Come on out and meet the rest of the family," encouraged Roger at the end of our first conversation. He was action-oriented and engaged.

When I met with the rest of the family, everyone expressed openness and enthusiasm for putting a framework in place to guide the family's future. I proposed a process to develop a family constitution, which included completing the family survey, and this would be followed by individual meetings with each family member. Then I would prepare an outline for an agreement. We'd discuss this outline together at a family meeting.

"Let's get started," said Roger when he called to share the family's decision. "My mom and sisters are very excited too!"

"I'm ready to get more involved," shared Sally, a daughter in her twenties. We met over brunch in the local café in the college town where she lived with her husband and son. "Except I don't know what to do. Since I don't work in the family business, and I have a young child at home, I'm not sure what my role is. Maybe I can help organize the meetings or be involved in philanthropy." As is often the case for family members who don't work in the business, she was eager to find her place.

Tanya, a daughter also in her twenties, is a busy teacher who lives several time zones away and found the family meetings frustrating. "We talk about the same things over and over again at every meeting, but we never seem to make any decisions. We need to move forward with the topics on the docket."

Like many moms, Beth wanted to be sure everyone was getting along. "I'm relieved that you're going to help us so I can stop worrying. We need to make some decisions about the family and the business."

"Tell me more," I urged. I wanted to hear what was really on Beth's mind.

"Bill is in denial about planning for the future of the business. He thinks Roger's going to run it, but I don't think Roger wants it. He needs to do his own thing. And then there's Roger; no one knows what he's doing or how much he's spending in the family office."

Bill and I met for dinner. He was a natural salesman and beamed with pride in his work. "I just love the business. I'm still on fire about it every day." Bill was eager to talk about the special niche his company served in the market.

"We've made money, but that doesn't mean we should change our ways. Being frugal got us here, and I want to keep it that way."

When I asked Bill about his thoughts about his family, he seemed proud and happy and not inclined to worry too much about the future. "Our kids will be fine. I wish Beth understood money better, but that's not what she does."

It was an opportune time for the family members to define their values, develop a mission statement, and determine how the family would make decisions as it was growing. The core family "team" included the parents and three adult children who are all at the early stages of building their own families. With a thriving company, family office, and positive relationships connecting them, a more defined governance plan was the natural next step.

Everyone was on board, but every family member also had questions about the future. "How will spouses be involved?" wondered Tanya. "What about our kids working in the family business?" asked Sally. "We need to make sure everyone understands the family's finances," Roger urged.

This business-owning family had already articulated values to guide interactions with employees and customers: honest, dependable, competent, supportive, and intelligent. The family members understood the importance of principles, so they were very interested in completing the family survey to help them adapt this same way of thinking to their family.

Roger and I tailored several of the survey questions to the particular needs of this family. We agreed to start by identifying the members' personal values as well as their *family* values, both those that exist today as well as aspirational values that the family believes are important for its future success. Family stories and memories would be there too. It would all be tied together in the constitution.

The survey responses showed that the values of the individuals were in sync with those of the family as a whole. Family members identified a number of common principles. These shared core values provided a solid foundation for developing the framework of the family agreement. This is where the family's personality shines through (see figure 6.1).

When family members were asked to compare the existing values of the family as a whole with those they believed to be important for long-term family success, the responses showed that there was more work to do. As is often the case, family members wanted more open communication with greater honesty and candor (see figure 6.2).

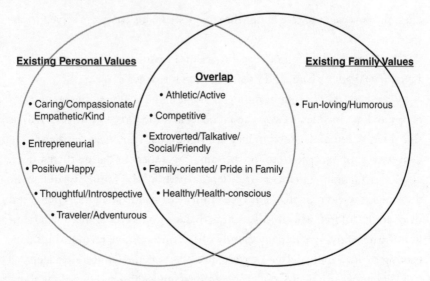

Figure 6.1 Overlap Between Existing Personal Values and Existing Family Values.

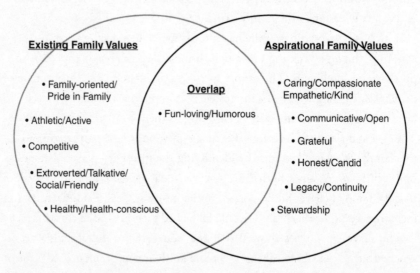

Figure 6.2 Overlap Between Existing Family Values and Aspirational Family Values.

At the same time, family members expressed unanimous agreement about their interest in working together as stewards of the family and its wealth. They had already begun to have regular family meetings, so their "family team" had established a good foundation of trust from which to build its decision-making process (see figure 6.3).

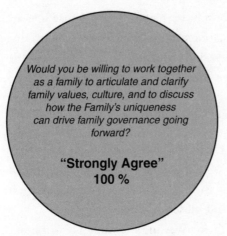

Would you be willing to work together
as a family to articulate and clarify
family values, culture, and to discuss
how the Family's uniqueness
can drive family governance going
forward?

**"Strongly Agree"
100 %**

Figure 6.3   Family Agreement to Work Together.

With shared values (see figure 6.1) and aspirational goals (see figure 6.2) identified, the next step was for the family to begin working together to write its mission statement (see figure 6.3). The following survey question spurred ideas and discussion: "How would you describe the family's fundamental purpose and philosophy?"

The family members agreed on their mission: *"To continually educate, grow, and encourage the success of our family members over time. To diversify and expand our family enterprise while maintaining our core values. To balance where we came from with where we are going."*

Survey questions about decision making and communication raised a number of questions that were on the minds of the family members and that would be the building blocks for the family constitution.

- How does the family make decisions?
- What is the succession plan for the family business?
- How are decisions made about joint family investments?
- How can we provide financial education to family members?
- Who attends the family meetings? Spouses? Children? Do they vote?
- What are the rules and expectations for family members working in the business?
- Does the family want to be involved in philanthropy? If so, what and how?
- What is the job description for the head of the family office?

- Who is responsible for planning family meetings and retreats?
- What information should be communicated to shareholders about the family business and the family office?
- How does the family resolve conflicts?

Writing the Family Constitution

Every family that develops a constitution will have issues unique to its culture and circumstances. At the same time, many families face similar questions. As families develop their own document, they can learn from the experiences of other families and those who advise them.

According to Taylor Wessing's "Family Constitution Guide," the family constitution will "set out broad principles in a number of areas, such as education, communication, the scope and use of the family office, [and] expenditure on joint and individual projects. It will usually define the persons having particular roles in relation to the family business, the family office, or family trusts. It can also include specific policies on matters such as investment, education, [or] employment by the family business."[3]

Family governance experts Daniela Montemerlo and John Ward suggest that a constitution include the following components:

- Preamble or introduction (Who?)
- Statement of family values and beliefs (Why?)
- Outline of family business principles (What?)
- Policies that govern family and business relations (How?)
- Conclusion on the method to make amendments (When?)[4]

* * *

After considering the family's specific questions and input as well as best practices for family constitutions, such as those described above, we developed a template for a constitution for Roger's family. The family approved the template and provided additional input regarding specific policies. Then it was time for the family to discuss its specific philosophy.

Over the next six months, the family drafted the policies and approved the constitution. The members appointed the family council to oversee the family governance and agreed on a timetable for implementing the policies. The family council decided to meet twice each year and agreed on a leader who would coordinate meetings and agendas. The board of directors and the family council would coordinate meeting and communication schedules. The family agreed to review the constitution annually to ensure it would remain effective.

* * *

Family Constitution Outline

Introduction

- Purpose of the agreement
- Subjects covered
- Signers of the agreement
- Family background

Family Philosophy

- Mission statement
- Family values
- Family business ownership
- Family philanthropy

Business Philosophy

- Company mission statement
- Company values
- Shareholders' principles

Family Governance Policies

- Family council
- Family meetings and retreats
- Family office
- Family education
- Communication

Business Governance Policies

- Board of directors
- CEO succession
- Shareholders' rights and responsibilities
- Family members working in the company

The Constitution

- Amending the agreement

* * *

Developing a constitution provides the family with much more than just a document to share. Offering input, raising questions, and participating in the dialogue all offer opportunities for family members to engage with each other in meaningful ways regarding the future of their family. The process itself builds communication and trust.

Well-run companies appreciate that no one person has all the best answers. They analyze, discuss, and look ahead to the future before acting. Families should also have a way to share information when they make decisions. Whether in a business or a family, being heard is a right and a privilege for each person. When members know why they are important to how the family runs, they stay motivated.

Today's families are poised to benefit from the ongoing forum for dialogue that family meetings provide. Two powerful generations, baby boomers and millennials, are well suited to work together as their families prepare to transition leadership and wealth. The baby boomers who have accumulated wealth are now turning inward in search of personal growth and meaningful experiences. The millennials have grown up in an age of connectivity and are not only comfortable with but crave today's sharing economy.

Authenticity, sustainability, and giving back are common values that connect these two generations and that lead naturally back to the family as a connection point. These generations are driven not by a sense of how to accumulate more things but how to have more experiences and achieve personal growth. Families that engage in these conversations between the generations can use written agreements as a tool to unite the members.

Whether it's one page or many, having a written family document gives the family staying power. When the members draft it, debate it, and adopt it, they can depend on it. Everyone shares, and everyone signs. Just like any constitution, the family document can be amended at any time.

Family Investing Is More Sense
Than Dollars

CHAPTER 7

Family IQ: Education and Training

A n educated workforce is crucial to fueling growth. Training employees improves performance, which adds to the bottom line. Companies understand that human capital is their greatest asset. The same is true for families.

In 2013, spending on corporate professional development grew by 15 percent to $70 billion in the United States and $130 billion worldwide.[1] With global leadership gaps one of the most pressing concerns on the minds of business leaders, companies are investing more than ever in leadership and management education. Families face the same demographic trends as aging baby boomers consider the readiness of the next generation to become the stewards of family wealth.

Leading businesses have designed special programs to provide the education their employees need, and to encourage the best talent to remain with their organizations. One industry giant, United Technologies, has spent over $1 billion through the company's Employee Scholars Program. It pays up front for tuition, books, and fees for a degree of the employee's choice. UPS has enrolled over 113,000 employees in its Tuition Assistance Program.[2] These workers are more likely to advance within the ranks of their companies and remain with the firms longer. Families also benefit from educating their members, but it's not always about academics.

Companies recognize that while they must recruit the next generation of corporate leaders, younger professionals have different expectations for how they will lead. Deloitte's Global Millennial Research study found that millennials are already eager to assume more responsibilities, that they thrive on innovation and change, and that they value open and inclusive styles.[3] When families harness this energy effectively they have the potential for adding great bench strength to their own teams.

With an unprecedented level of wealth transfer underway, it is more important than ever for families to prepare their heirs for the successful transition of wealth and the continuity of the family. A 2014 study released by the Center on Wealth and Philanthropy at Boston College estimated that $59 trillion will be transferred from over 93 million American estates between 2007 and 2061 to heirs, estate taxes, and charities.[4] Those who receive these new resources have a tremendous opportunity to positively impact their families and communities.

As talented and motivated as they are, members of the next generation still need to be properly prepared for the positions of influence they will soon hold. Financial acumen is at the top of the list of what they need. A family with a strategic plan, with its mission, values, goals, and governance systems in place, is the ideal training ground. Most parents will gladly pay for tutors or extracurricular activities to prepare their children to do well in school. Research indicates that $2.5 billion is spent per year on test preparation services alone.[5] However, most financial education is left to chance or ignored altogether. This is a gamble families can't afford to take.

Our current educational system lacks any systematic approach to money management in school curricula. During Global Money Week in March 2014, the Central Bank of Nigeria announced that financial literacy will be included in the school curricula beginning in 2015. The United Kingdom incorporated financial education in the national curriculum in 2013 with classes in financial mathematics to teach students to manage money and plan for future financial decisions.[6] These are hopeful signs on the global scene, but the new initiatives aren't of any help to the young people who are already completing their traditional education and entering adulthood. Thus far, there is no such effort underway on any large scale in the United States.

This leaves the job squarely in the hands of families.

Financial education experts remind us that there are no quick fixes to mastering money skills. Joline Godfrey, CEO of Independent Means, a firm she founded to teach kids money skills, designed the "drip, drip, drip" approach to financial education, which argues that financial consciousness and skills are best developed over time.[7] Elaine King Fuentes, director of Education and Family Governance at WE Family Offices, also argues for a long-term approach that teaches the value of a dollar, the importance of savings, the basics of investing, and the exponential effect of giving back.[8] These are habits best learned and reinforced with a family strategy.

Just as companies require employees to acquire new skills in our rapidly changing global economy, families must set financial literacy as an expectation for their members. Just as employers provide tools and incentives to motivate workers to make the most of their careers and contribute to their firm's success, families should provide financial skills to their members just as they do other educational resources. Many would like to do this, but it is challenging to create a program from scratch.

That's why one of our clients called me for help.

Financial Education 101: It Takes More than a Debit Card

"Thank you for coming up," said Barbara, welcoming me to tea at her peaceful lakeside home. We sat down together in her den, surrounded by shelves of books and tasteful art, and she continued, "I've been thinking about those trust funds that will go to my grandchildren one day. Those girls are getting older, and so am I. I'd like to talk about how we can be sure they are prepared to manage things when the time comes."

When Barbara Barnes said she wanted to see me, I knew something important was on her mind. She had been a client of our firm for many years. Her own financial plans were in solid shape. Now in her late seventies, she had always had a good head for money.

Like most people, she had faced her own difficulties, including the death of her husband, and concerns about some of the decisions her children had made over the years. Her grandchildren were her pride and joy. Her estate plan was organized to leave them substantial sums and leave funds for her favorite charities. As they were approaching adulthood, she was starting to wonder.

"As you know, my four grandchildren mean the world to me. I have always hoped that the funds I would be able to leave them would help them to lead just as nice a life as I've been fortunate to have. But I was lucky. I learned about the value of money from my father, who always talked with me about stocks. These are nice young people, but they haven't had the same exposure to finance that I had."

"I know how close you have always been to your grandchildren. We'd be glad to work with them. We have a financial workshop designed for this age group that they could attend together. That will help us determine what they know already and what they might need in the future. Most important, we'll be a resource for them when they need one."

We agreed that Barbara would write a letter to her grandchildren to let them know of her desire for them to learn financial skills. She would introduce me, and I would follow up to arrange for the session. She could be the catalyst but didn't need to do all the hands-on teaching.

The four cousins arrived in my office in good spirits one summer afternoon, somewhat unsure of what was in store, knowing only that their grandmother was behind the idea. These young people were lucky. They had been to excellent schools, and all four were in college and doing well. One was headed to Europe for a semester of study, and another had just completed a summer internship at an advertising agency. The other two had worked on a ranch together in Wyoming.

We began the session by chatting together informally. Building rapport was the first step. They weren't looking for lectures. We wanted to focus the discussion at a level appropriate to their knowledge. We gathered in our conference room with presentation books for each participant. It was a professional meeting with an educational approach.

"Tell me a little about your interests and plans," I began. "What's on your mind as you think about your future? Is there anything about money that you'd like to know more about?"

"I'm an economics major. I like it, but I don't really know what's next after college," said Emily. "I am interested in learning more about investing."

"I know I need to manage my money better," said Jill, "and I know I probably lose track of expenses. I have lots of dinners out with my friends, and I buy things, but I really don't keep track of exactly what I spend."

"I just call my parents and they take care of it," said Caroline. "I have a credit card that goes to them."

"I'm interested in getting a job in marketing or public relations," said Julie. "I had an internship this summer with a public relations firm, so I hope I can work for them next year after I graduate. I would like to take the summer off to travel after I graduate."

The program we designed was meant to encourage the younger generation to think more about the practical side of making financial decisions. A budgeting exercise included the kinds of salaries to expect for different jobs and how much it costs to live independently. Reviewing an actual check stub showed them how much of the monthly paycheck goes to taxes. Spending, saving, investing, and giving something to charity was all a part of the activity that morning, just as it would be in real life.

"Oops, I ran out of money before I paid for all of my stuff," admitted Julie as she completed the budget exercise. "But I see if I picked a less expensive car then I could make it work."

"My budget turned out okay, but I didn't have much left over. This is the first time I've actually added up how much everything costs," commented Caroline, somewhat nervously.

A peek into the how-tos of banking, credit cards, FICO scores, and 401(k) plans introduced practical concepts and a new vocabulary. We discussed the difference between saving and investing and the need for an emergency fund. It was financial fitness 101.

"I had no idea that there was anything wrong with just paying the minimum amount on my credit card. I knew the interest rates were high, but I never really thought about how much more that would cost," said Jill. "If I charged $100 each year and only paid the minimum due, it would cost me $2,500 in ten years! That's crazy." We provided them with a chart to illustrate the financial impact of not handling credit cards properly (see figure 7.1).

"Much better to invest your money, so let's talk about that," I suggested.

"My grandmother likes the stock market," commented Emily. "How can I learn more about it?"

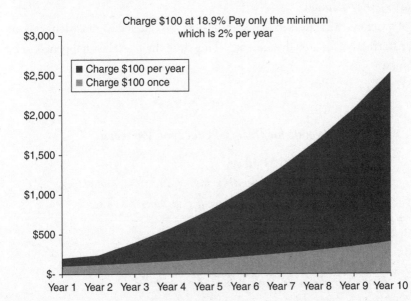

Figure 7.1 Cost of Credit Card Debt.

"Of course, you can continue to read and follow the financial markets on your own, but another idea is to join the student investment fund at your college," I suggested. "You would have the opportunity to learn with some of your fellow students."

The session brought financial theory closer to home. Our goal was to help Barbara's grandkids to focus on the fact that money choices matter. One size doesn't fit all when it comes to the best preparation for jobs, but no matter the career, money skills are a necessity to make it work.

We concluded the session with gifts—two of my favorite books, with our business cards tucked inside. One closing piece of advice was: "Find a financial mentor, someone you can call on when you have questions about money. We all need help from time to time."

Several months later, I received an e-mail from Julie. "Mrs. Taylor, may we set up a time to talk about my college account? I want to review how much money I have spent and how to plan my budget for the rest of the year."

When Julie and I reviewed her finances, the stocks and bonds she had been learning about became more relevant to her than ticker symbols on a brokerage statement. She was connecting managing her money with managing her life.

The seeds had been planted and were starting to take root. As I've seen many times with members of the next generation, when encouraged and trusted, they respond.

Awareness was awakened. A mind-set was altered. Education can be transformative for a ready audience. This time the topic just happened to be money.

* * *

Agenda for Financial Education Workshop

1. Develop a Financial Mind-set
   Making decisions about spending, saving, investing, and giving.
   Choose a job and a lifestyle and see if your budget balances.
2. Practice Good Habits in College
   What do you need to know about banking?
   What is a credit score, and why does it matter?
   How do credit cards work? What are the pitfalls?
   What is "good debt" compared to "bad debt"?

3. Build a Financial Resume
   Tips for getting internships
   What is the best path to your career?
4. Establishing Professional Networks:
   What contacts do you have and how can you use them effectively?
5. Working with Mentors: The Wisdom of Good Advice
   What is a mentor and why do you need one?
8. Plan Ahead: Understanding Your Skills and Talents
   What is your value proposition?
   Do you need more training? Graduate school?
   What is your human, intellectual, and social capital?
9. Living within a Budget: Needs, Wants, *and* Savings
   What's in a paycheck? What's left after taxes? How much should you save?
10. Investing 101
    Stocks, bonds, and the Rule of 72
    Glossary of investment terms

* * *

All young people are concerned about success, and those from affluent families are no exception. With all their advantages, they still worry whether they have what it takes to make it in today's competitive world. The fact is that these kids have more resources at their disposal than money. It's their other "capital" that can be put to work to build a productive future.

Human, social, and intellectual capital are investments that only families can make in each other. Values, ethics, family history, and legacy build confidence. This is human capital. Friends, classmates, and coworkers provide the social network that sustains individuals for a lifetime. This is social capital. Skills, knowledge, information, and experience are intellectual capital to build one's future. Money is the financial capital that supports the rest. It's important too, of course, but it can be replaced more easily than the other kinds of capital.

As with any educational endeavor, financial skills take time to learn. Family meetings are a great time to reinforce good habits and introduce more advanced concepts. Financial reports from the family business, charitable fund brokerage statements, or college savings accounts can all be used to teach the basic vocabulary of finance and investing.

When members share ownership in a family asset, their bonds are more than personal. They're financial. Everyone has a job to do to keep the family dynamic healthy and the business dynamic professional. Education can make the family partnership a blessing instead of a curse. Everyone doesn't need to become an expert, but all family members need to know what the expert is talking about.

* * *

It's not only members of the younger generation who need money skills. An education gap also exists when it comes to women's mastery of financial information. Since women control more than 60 percent of the private wealth in the United States and make 80 percent of all purchases, it is no secret that women's financial influence is significant. At the same time, in 59 percent of marriages, the husband makes all the investment decisions. A study discovered that only 53 percent of women said they have the confidence to invest, compared to 82 percent of men.[9]

Events in women's lives underscore the likelihood that we will not only earn money but will need to manage it as well. Consider the following statistics: women live an average of five to ten years longer than men; over 30 percent of marriages end in divorce, and 80 percent of men die married, while 80 percent of women die single. Altogether, these trends lead to a staggering outcome: at some point 95 percent of all women are likely to become solely responsible for managing their finances.[10]

Even though the statistics about women inheriting the investment responsibility should be compelling enough on their own, connecting finances to life's real opportunities and challenges brings the theory close to home. Having good money skills contributes to making sound decisions throughout life. Each phase of life brings choices with financial consequences.

The first phase, which I call "Establishing Roots," includes building a career, purchasing a home, and starting a family. Even the most highly educated and capable women aren't always as proactive as they should be in dealing with relationships and money. Old cultural habits can still be hard to break.

A young attorney came to see me with a dilemma. She was from a well-to-do family and was fortunate not to be burdened by student loans or other debt. She had a great education and was beginning a promising career. But she and her new husband had different financial habits.

"My husband and I can't discuss our finances without stress. He is an artist and doesn't have a large income. He has student loan debt, but he keeps spending on other things. It seems like he's always buying things we don't need. I just discovered he has a lot of credit card debt too," she explained.

I counseled this young couple and helped the two devise a budget and a plan. We met every few months so they would have a sounding board as well as accountability to stay on track. Talking about money wasn't easy for these two, but with practice they got better at it.

As women enter midlife and reach prime earning capacity, many enter a second phase. I refer to this as the sandwich generation; this phase brings college costs, aging parents, and the possibility of life events that can change a person's economic destiny. Even women who have enjoyed financial security can be devastated by the financial impact of sudden changes. These events may include divorce, widowhood, or illness. This is when money skills are most needed but all too often women aren't ready when the "Big One" strikes.

My Husband Handled the Money

Susan's friend Jane suggested she call me. She arrived in my office with several boxes of paperwork. Tears soon filled her clear blue eyes.

"I don't know how all this got away from me. My husband passed away two months ago. He always handled our finances, and over the years we got involved in more investments. Now I keep finding more and more that I didn't know he was doing. He made some bad decisions toward the end. I knew he was ill, but I just couldn't take the money management away from him."

Susan's husband had made some risky investments, but fortunately they weren't devastating. Her financial future was not in jeopardy, but her lack of exposure to the family's finances caused her additional emotional stress at a time when she was least prepared to cope with it. I helped her organize the administrative jumble and began a methodical process of assessing the investments. Susan was a bright woman and soon developed confidence about what she owned and how the investments worked. As I experience so often with women like Susan, she had good instincts and could manage her finances quite capably once she understood them.

Over the next year Susan and I worked closely with her attorney and accountant as a team to advise her as she assumed the new role of CEO, chief economic officer, for her own life. She delegated the work to us but owned the responsibility for herself. She learned the language of finance, considered her options, and moved forward.

"I feel so much better about this part of my life," Susan remarked a few years later. "Of course, I miss my husband terribly, but I know that financially I'll be fine."

Widows don't have to go through the stress of financial uncertainty at the same time they also experience emotional loss. Financial education is something all women should master.

* * *

After the sandwich generation, when so much attention is often placed on others, women can look forward to realizing personal dreams. Those with economic independence can imagine an exciting time, a time I suggest that can be a kind of "Revolutionary Retirement" during which those who are financially strong can positively impact their families, communities, and their own personal aspirations with their financial resources. The ultimate satisfaction of a life well lived for many includes the gift of creating a legacy through sustaining family values, raising financially secure children and grandchildren, and improving our communities through philanthropic works.

To realize our financial potential, women must become financially fit. I offer five steps as a checkup for financial fitness. No matter how much money we have, circumstances can change. Peace of mind about money increases with knowledge.

* * *

Financial Fitness Check List

1. Know your assets: What do you own? This includes business interests, real estate, cash, stocks, bonds, and other investments. It also means having the documents organized and accessible. Read your brokerage statements and meet regularly with your financial advisor.
2. What is your income and how much do you spend? What money comes in from all sources and what are your total expenses each year? Be familiar with your tax situation and tax advisor. Never sign anything you don't understand.

3. How could your income and financial position change over time? Know the risks and potential rewards of your particular situation.
4. Separate your needs from your wants. This gives you flexibility should you need it.
5. Keep an adequate safety net in case financial circumstances change. This should be readily available in case of emergencies or unexpected expenses. Many advisors recommend at least six months, but maybe more, depending upon your situation.

* * *

These questions can form the basis for a meeting with a financial advisor to review one's financial fitness plans. There are no set answers to the questions, since everyone has different circumstances, responsibilities, and lifestyles. It is the advisor's responsibility to provide the information needed to be informed and comfortable with a financial strategy. It is *the family member's* responsibility to ask the questions and insist on a dialogue.

Even the most seasoned professionals can't predict with any certainty what is going to occur in the financial markets. But if family members understand their finances and operate with a margin of safety, they will be prepared to make decisions if and when changes come. It's important to stay informed, be aware, and keep learning.

CHAPTER 8

Family EQ: Getting Along to Get Ahead

What do Anna Nicole Smith, Leona Helmsley, Brooke Astor, and Jay Pritzker have in common?

They are all famous people associated with family fights over money. Although these are notorious headline stories that most people will never experience, many families are torn apart by disagreements over inheritances. In a 2011 study by Barclays Wealth Insights, 40 percent of 2,000 global families responded that they have had direct involvement in wealth transfers leading to disputes[1]; clearly, such family conflicts aren't all that rare.

Experts point to a lack of communication within the family as the cause of the discord. The Williams Group study of 2003 found that 60 percent of the failures in wealth transfer were caused by a breakdown of communications and trust.[2] Current research indicates that these challenges continue. When families put off talking about money, the older members become more hesitant to address the topic, and the younger members remain unprepared for what's ahead. Secrecy is an enemy of trust.

The Barclays study found that 34 percent of the wealthy parents in the study were ambivalent or did not trust their children to protect their inheritance.[3] Spending habits can be suspect. Work ethics can be different. Privilege can breed entitlement. "I'm disinheriting her," can be more than an idle threat once trust is broken. Despite all the technology that keeps us connected, we're still not really in touch about money.

Business leaders understand that effective collaboration is vital to a company's success. KPMG's Centre for Family Business views communication as a risk-management strategy. Talking about money matters nips potential issues in the bud. Working together creates solutions. When families get communication and cooperation right, their bonds help to solve problems instead of creating more. These advisors suggest that the natural advantages that business families have in terms of their potential for long-term success can become a disadvantage when communication is poor.[4]

The good news is that forging dialogue in families is within our control. As with many challenges, the solution seems simple but is tough to bring about. It takes openness and candor. Communication is the ultimate two-way street.

When it comes to talking about money, the consequences of not doing it well can be dire. A family's ties are more fragile than its fortunes. Dianne's story tells this tale all too well.

Money Secrets Don't Lie

"Mom, is there anything I can do to help you and Dad organize your finances?" offered Dianne, as she had done frequently over the years. Dianne was the ideal family member to help her parents. She earned both her CPA and the CFA and is a financial professional.

"I know you're on top of your bills, but maybe I can mechanize things and make them easier to keep track of," she offered gently. Dianne knew her parents were very proud of her accomplishments, but they also valued their privacy. She wanted to show them the respect she felt they deserved, but she also recognized they were getting older and might benefit from her skills.

"No, thank you, dear. We're doing just fine."

That was the response she'd received consistently. It was always delivered pleasantly, but firmly. They had a system. Her dad was a product of his generation. He earned the money and handed everything over to his wife, who paid the bills and handled the day-to-day finances.

Then his wife passed away suddenly. The day after the funeral, a grieving Dianne sat down at her mother's desk to open the mail to see what needed to be done to help her father tackle the finances. She was stunned by what she found.

"Dad, do you and Mom still have a mortgage on the house?" Dianne asked as she examined the payment stub.

"No, we paid that off years ago," he told her with certainty.

Or so he thought. Dianne began looking through all the desk drawers and was shocked to find stacks of envelopes, still sealed. Her father looked on, confused.

When she opened the phone bill, things became even murkier. The same number was called each day for under one minute. It was an automated account balance number for the checking account. Instead of balancing the checkbook, her mother had called the bank each day to find out how much was in the account. Then, she would write a check to pay the most overdue bills. Dianne's heart sank.

Concern growing, Dianne said, "Dad, we need to look through the other places where Mom might have kept old paperwork, mail, and so on."

They quickly uncovered years of unopened mail. Bank statements revealed mounting overdraft fees, monthly charges for vendors that had not been used for years, all resulting in a gradual depletion of the couple's cash. There were no savings left at all.

Dianne understood all too well what this meant. "Dad, I'm going to get to the bottom of all this. The finances aren't as organized as I thought they were."

"Can you just make sure I can stay here in our house?"

He had no idea what he was asking of his daughter. As capable as Dianne was financially, it was overwhelming to deal with the grief of losing her mother, only to discover their financial life was in a shambles.

"Dad, you have to do exactly as I say from now on." He didn't ask any questions.

Seven years later, Dianne was grateful to be able to utter the phrase, "Barring any unforeseen events, you'll be able to stay here until you're 99 years old, Dad."

"I'd like that," he said with a smile.

Dianne shared this story with me as we talked about how she could do things differently in her own family.

"Thanks to a strong stock market these last few years, I was able to build Dad's assets back. What if that hadn't been the case? It could have been devastating for a man who had worked so hard his whole life. I want to start educating my boys right away to increase their financial knowledge. And I want our family to talk about money, how we manage it at home and what it means to live within our means."

Dianne and I designed a plan for her sons as well as a money communication plan for her family. The boys got jobs when they turned sixteen and opened checking accounts. Over the summer, we met several times to talk about earning, saving, investing, and giving back, lessons learned with their own money.

During one session, we used the family's actual budget to teach them about tracking expenses and budgeting. The youngest boy, Brad, commented, "I had no idea what it took to run our family."

"Your mom and dad want you to understand how the finances work. While they hope that it is a long time down the road, one day you'll need to take over for your mom just as she did for her dad."

When we met recently to discuss the family's charitable gifts for the season, she confided, "I'll never know what happened with Mom and Dad's money. Even though I talked with her every single day, she made money off-limits. The bad experience I had when she died has had a silver lining," Dianne admitted. "I love the conversations that our family has now about money, not only about what we spend, but about what charities we want to support. I used to just make the decisions because it wasn't that much money. Now I know that the discussions themselves are just as important as writing the checks."

*　　*　　*

Communicating well requires a healthy dose of EQ as well as IQ.

EQ, also known as emotional intelligence quotient, is the ability to identify and manage your own emotions and the emotions of others. It is the ability to harness feelings and apply them to problem solving. In addition to regulating your own emotions, EQ enables you to work well with others in times of stress.[5]

When money is added to the equation, the dynamic can be exacerbated. EQ adds the empathy that's crucial for mutual understanding. The need is even greater when issues such as age, illness, disability, and family expectations enter the mix. IQ helps us make money. EQ helps us talk about it.

Tackling money topics is a tall order, but the subject must be addressed. Experts say that communicating intentions about the family wealth is healthy for all concerned. Respected psychologist and wealth advisor Lee Hausner recommends that "generally when parents inform their children about their estate plans, the children feel more respected. Lack of information can lead to misunderstandings about intentions and values."[6] Discussing the family's financial realities with adult children can not only solve immediate problems, it can temper long-term ill will due to surprises about the family's financial circumstances.

To avoid unnecessary glitches about money, take three steps:

1. Document what you have and how to access the funds, including passwords for online banking.
2. Discuss with your spouse or immediate kin what the specifics are with family finances and how the family budget is organized. If there are any financial arrangements that those who depend on you are not aware of, now is the time for candid conversations.
3. Make sure your plan is sustainable for you and those who depend on you in case you become ill or incapacitated.

If communicating is so good for us, why is it so hard to do? When it comes to estate planning, few want to confront their own mortality. For some, it's a matter of relinquishing control of an important part of their identities. Some parents worry that their children will lose their motivation to be productive if they know that a significant inheritance is in the offing. There's also the threat of stirring up family quarrels over who is getting what. Or who is not getting what.

Others simply live by the old adage "don't tell others what you have." For them, to do otherwise is just bad form. In Dianne's case, it was a more a matter of "don't tell others what you don't have." Whether it's for reasons of procrastination or privacy, there are plenty of barriers between family members and talking about their money.

If the conversations are handled well, the benefits of open dialogue about family wealth can outweigh the risks. The rewards are emotional as well as financial. When parents explain their plans ahead of time, everyone has the opportunity to ask questions, offer feedback, and plan accordingly. Sometimes new ideas or information come to light that result in a better solution. Even if resentments crop up, it's better to talk things out in advance than risk a lifetime of hurt feelings. As the famous line in the movie *The Godfather* goes, "Blood is a big expense."

Knowledge always trumps ignorance. In a profound change from past generations, when the patriarch would pass away and his wishes would be revealed to expectant heirs at the proverbial "reading of the will," families of today can watch the seeds they have sown bear fruit in their own lifetimes. Transparency is just as good for families as it is for businesses.

The Dixon family discovered this when they started the dialogue at their annual retreat.

Let's Talk

"It's wonderful to have everyone together again like this," began Kathy as the group settled into their comfortable chairs, ready to begin their summer retreat. The weathered beach house where they gathered was like an old family friend. Ocean breezes wafted in gently, creating a relaxed atmosphere. It was the third time the thirteen members of the family had gathered together for a family meeting. As had become their custom, Kathy and Bob invited their three children, their spouses, and the grandchildren aged sixteen and older to attend the discussions.

"It was a fun dinner last night," Kathy continued. "The cruise around the harbor was the perfect way to start our weekend together. A special thanks to Jack for arranging the music trio. Grandma Sarah would have loved it. Since Betsy and Rob are new to the retreat this year, would someone tell them the story?"

"I will," offered Bill, a son who had been particularly close to his grandmother. "After she passed away, we decided to do something to honor her. Since she loved music so much, we decided to make a gift to the local symphony. The musicians who played for us last night were from the group. They loved her too and were happy to play some of her favorite pieces for us."

Touched, Kathy gave him a hug. "That's a nice way to start our meeting. It's a reminder of how grateful we are for Grandma and Granddad's hard work all those years. And that being generous is one of the things we all decided is important to us as a family. We also decided we wanted to open a dialogue within the family. So Bob and I think that it's a good time to talk with you about some of the plans we've made to take care of our affairs after we're gone. Naturally, we hope that's a long time from now, but one thing Grandma and Granddad always said was 'Better safe than sorry.'"

Bob chimed in, "You all mean the world to Kathy and me. We've done a lot of thinking about how to make sure each of you and the causes we care about are provided for. Part of the responsibility of having financial good fortune is to make sure everything is organized so that there aren't any mix-ups later. We've asked our trusted advisor, Ms. Taylor, to join us for the conversation," she said as she introduced me.

"I'm so honored to be here," I began. "I have worked with Kathy and Bob for several years now to help them with the plans that reflect their values and provide for all of you. I've encouraged them to share things with you, and our job is to explain the process and answer any questions."

My role was to make sure that family members understood the plan and, more important, to encourage discussion. I walked the family through a diagram that showed the diverse assets that Bob and Kathy own and how the trusts that hold the funds have been managed through the years.

"Bob and Kathy have made sure their affairs are in good order now and in the future. They learned this from their parents, and one day the good fortune and responsibility will be yours. They hope these funds can be passed on for generations to come," I explained.

Their son, Bill, raised his hand, "Grandma and Granddad saved all this?"

"Yes, that's right, Bill," I replied. "They were hard working and thrifty and generous. Your parents have the same philosophy and would like to do everything they can to have you understand their perspective. They think of it not as 'their money,' but the 'family's money.' It's to support the values the family set down together in your early meetings, such as encouraging the entrepreneurial spirit of a promising new business. It's about investing in the family's progress. But it's not for frivolous spending."

"So you and Dad think of this kind of like having a family bank? There's more there, but when you spend it you need to think about replacing it?" Bill inquired with a grin.

"Yes, that's exactly right, although we never really thought about it in those terms. Your Grandma and Granddad had a comfortable life, and they wanted to share that with future family members. It's a frugal philosophy that's worked out well for the family over the years," Kathy responded.

"It's a matter of thinking about continuing our family. You and your families will benefit, and so will those members that follow you all. There are some conditions. As you kids already know, if there's a divorce, the family money is protected. It stays with the family. That was all taken care of months before each of you married. We just thought now was the right time to let you know more about what was behind that plan. "

The kids were quiet. "I know this can be uncomfortable, but it's not meant to be personal. We love our daughters and son-in-law dearly. And of course we hope we're all together for years and years to come," said Bob. "I'm glad we started this conversation today, so that you all can have time to digest it. Talking about things honestly. That's the most important thing."

This family learned that discussions about money don't have to be confrontational. Differences of opinion are par for the course when it comes to touchy subjects. Members may not always agree on an outcome, but candid communication helps them accept the answers.

* * *

In today's increasingly mobile world, our spheres of influence extend far and wide. This is true for global businesses as well as for multigenerational families. Whether it's a company's employees or a family's members, people are now accustomed having to instant information and fast feedback.

It's more important than ever to calibrate our communication to the audience. According to former Oracle and SAP executive Heather Zynczak, global companies face four major communications challenges.[7]

1. Lack of clarity: Communication doesn't always sink in the first time around with a diverse group of people who are often multitasking during meetings.
   Remedy: Put action items and key decisions in writing.

2. Slow decision making: Coordinating priorities of many people in different locations means things take longer to get scheduled and completed.
   Remedy: Communicate strategy and direction face-to-face.

3. Disjointed conflict resolution: Delicate situations with tough issues are hard to manage, especially when people aren't meeting face-to-face.
   Remedy: Pick up the phone. Never communicate tough messages via e-mail.

4. Great company culture is difficult to define and achieve and takes consistent team building and bonding.
   Remedy: Invest in cultural training.

These points ring true for diverse, growing families as well. Communication glitches can cause tensions in families just as they do in businesses. There are many kinds of families and many kinds of companies. Poor communication knows no boundaries. It can bring even the biggest and best to the brink.

For example, after the blowout of the Deepwater Horizon oil rig in 2010, BP found itself in a huge crisis. According to a White House commission report, "poor communications" and a failure to "share important information" were to blame. Similarly, at Enron, a study of the causes of the collapse pointed to the failure of senior managers to "communicate appropriate values" and "maintain openness to signs of problems." Likewise, Nokia missed its industry's big move to smartphones because of "habits of communication that favored unfocused discussions about strategy."[8]

Businesses and families alike usually recognize the risks of poor financial management, but they don't always see the dangers of poor communications management. When business leaders champion open dialogue as key to the company's strategy, people engage. A culture of communication keeps people close to the cause that unites them. And that's how they stay connected.

A communications plan only works if people use it. A family with its strategy in place has a system. Then it needs to practice. The questions don't have to be complicated, but they have to be answered.

1. **Who are we?** Collaborating to define the family's purpose with a written mission statement sets the stage for a strong culture of teamwork. *Repeat the mission and retell the family stories. Write them down. Pass them around.*

2. **What's important to us?** Keeping values at the top of everyone's mind clarifies decision making and priorities. *When challenges arise, go back to the core values. Are we in sync with our principles?*

3. **What do we believe?** Looking to the family agreement for guidance and direction about philosophy and policies calms the waters during times of change or conflict. *What did our predecessors think? Is there a better way?*

4. **How do we stay connected?** Regular in-person family meetings that educate and energize are essential. *Are we still learning? Are we having fun?*

A family that is purposeful about its mission and values has already decided what is most important. If it has been working as a team to set goals and celebrate milestones, it knows what it is trying to accomplish. If it has a written family agreement, it has its principles and philosophy laid out to guide its actions. This kind of practice pays off.

*   *   *

Technology in the twenty-first century can make it seem as though we've bridged all our communication gaps. There's never a day without computers, mobile phones, e-mail, and chat rooms to keep things moving. There's a place for all this technology when we need to speed things up. To keep family ties meaningful, sometimes a family's best bet is to slow things down.

There's no substitute for togetherness. There's no better way than talking. It's time to start.

CHAPTER 9

Family Audit: Guidance and Mentoring

For Oprah Winfrey, it was Mrs. Duncan, her fourth-grade teacher. For Bill Clinton, it was his grandmother. For Mark Zuckerberg, it was Steve Jobs. For Warren Buffett, it was Benjamin Graham, another great investor and Buffett's university professor. Famous people often credit mentors with helping them succeed. Wisdom comes in many forms.

The original mentor was a character in Homer's epic poem *The Odyssey*. When Odysseus, the king of Ithaca, went to fight in the Trojan War, he entrusted the care and teaching of his son, Telemachus, to Mentor. Since the days of ancient Greece, the role of a mentor has been to impart spiritual, social, and personal values to the young. For families, sharing knowledge with the next generation is just as important now as it was centuries ago.

Seventy-one percent of Fortune 500 companies offer mentoring to their employees. Corporate leaders believe that using their own internal resources to develop up-and-comers is a wise strategy. The initial investment in coaching is returned sevenfold.[1] The evidence shows experience pays off in business. Role models are equally invaluable for families.

The terms "coach" and "mentor" are often used interchangeably, but the two have different responsibilities. Coaching is about improving performance in a specific area by developing certain skills. It's short-term and focused. Mentoring helps someone prepare to take on new responsibilities, work in a new environment, or build confidence to continue to learn and grow. Mentoring looks further down the road. There's a place for both coaching and mentoring at home.

Noted advisor James E. Hughes brings the concepts closer to the context of family in his writings on the subject. "Mentoring is about asking questions not about giving answers. A mentor's questions should guide us to the deepest possible learning about ourselves. Successful mentoring is a dialogue where both parties learn something essential."[2] This suggests a genuine partnership is formed. When you are looking for a mentor, it's smart to start with your family.

If family members are in business together, the case for mentoring is clear. KPMG's family business expert Christophe Bernard cites four ways in which mentoring the next generation contributes to the success of the family firm:

1. Creates a succession road map
2. Develops key business competencies
3. Encourages personal and business development
4. Embraces company values and vision[3]

When family members share ownership in a company, their bonds are more than emotional. They're financial. Everyone has a job to do to keep the family dynamic healthy and the business dynamic professional. There's a legacy to pass on and a business to run. This is a time when the family's elders can help.

It takes practice to forge the bonds of mentorship and requires a business-like approach with a personal touch. Mentorship is a chance to pay something forward.

Family Ties: Mentors at Work

The Anderson family of cousins gathered in the modest office in the small town where the company's operations were located. It was time for the annual shareholders' meeting of the Anderson Oil Company. Faded photographs of the fields in the early days lined the walls. Aside from the addition of a computer, nothing had changed much in the office since Bud Anderson set it up in the 1950s.

After Bud passed away, his son Don had called me for help as he and his siblings stepped up to be the new owners of the family company. A new agreement was put into place. Things ran smoothly for a long period of time. Ten years later, it was time for another transition.

"Welcome back home for our annual owners' meeting, everybody," began Don, who had been running the family company for the past decade. "It's an important day for our company. As everyone knows, I've been planning to step back from my role in managing the business. It's time to pass the torch to the next generation."

Eight cousins, ranging in age from twenty-two to forty, sat around the old oak table. Ever since they had been young children, the family had been holding annual meetings. Now that they were owners, the cousins paid close attention to the discussion.

In his characteristic modest but confident tone, Don continued, "Scott has been working alongside me for the last five years to prepare for taking the reins. Not only does he have the capabilities we need to continue to build the company, he's ready to dedicate his career to the family business. By mail ballot, all of the owners have agreed unanimously with his appointment as head of our company. Scott, congratulations! I couldn't be more confident about the future," Don beamed with pride.

"Thanks, Dad. I'm excited by this opportunity. I've learned so much from you. Granddad was my role model, too, and I saw firsthand what all this meant to him. I'll do my best to keep the family business strong," said Scott, his voice breaking with obvious emotion. He had been very close to his grandfather and was very sentimental about family ties.

Scott's mom, aunts, and uncles, who had watched Scott grow up, gave one another knowing glances and smiles. The younger generation sat quietly, not knowing what to do next. Sensing a room filled with emotion, I suggested gently, "Scott, I think everyone is looking forward to hearing how things have been going as you've worked more closely with your dad over the past year in preparation for this transition."

"Okay, everyone, let's go through our results from last year," continued Scott, the 36-year-old third-generation family member who would now run the oil and gas production company founded over sixty years ago by his grandfather. "So, all in all, we had a pretty good year," said Scott, as he concluded his presentation about the past year's results. "Prices were up. Production was up."

Scott's Uncle Jake, who had been an owner for many years, chimed in, "It's great that things have gone so well, but I remind everyone this is a risky business. It costs a bundle to drill a well, and often nothing comes of it. That's why I always save some dividends for when times get rough. Because they will," he cautioned.

One of the eldest cousins, Sue, was looking intently at the numbers and charts on the PowerPoint handout. "Do you think we're doing as well as the other businesses like ours in the area?"

"For our size, yes. That money we spent in the last two years to update our wells and do a little drilling has paid off. That's helped us increase production. Oil is a 'depleting asset.' We have to spend more to find more, because it will eventually run out. We just don't know exactly when. But it's a trade-off between distributing money to ourselves as owners and investing in the business for the future."

"What about next year?" asked Emily, another cousin, her hands folded in front of her. "I'd like to know what to expect so I can plan ahead."

Scott handed out another worksheet. "We'll take advantage of the spring months to do more drilling and repairs, so the budget you see provides for that. If prices hold, we should have similar results. Does anyone have any questions about next year's budget or about the monthly reports we've been sending?"

"I don't really know what to ask," admitted Lynne, Jake's daughter, another cousin of Scott's. As in every family, there was a wide range of knowledge about the business.

Sensing Lynne's interest but uncertainty at how to take the next step, I offered a comment, "That's completely understandable, Lynne. Scott is always available to meet individually with any of you to go over things."

"Maybe a trip out into the field would be a good thing for us to do. That way I can show you firsthand what we own and what we're doing," Scott suggested.

Everyone nodded, enthusiastic about the idea.

"I'd like to have a glossary of some sort that defines some of the industry lingo," suggested Carol, flipping through the pages of the handouts.

"Sure thing, we'll get that out to everyone," Scott promised.

"Scott, we all appreciate what you're doing. We love being a part of the business. It feels like family," said Emily. The youngest, Emily had always been one to offer a kind word of encouragement to others.

Like all small family businesses, this one had its share of ups and downs. But because the family members shared values and trust, the family business has weathered two generational transitions well. The leaders provided good information to fellow owners, and the owners were engaged and respectful. Good financial results have helped, but good family mentoring didn't hurt.

*   *   *

Families are awash in potential mentors. Parents, uncles, aunts, grandparents, cousins, siblings, advisors, business colleagues, and friends all can emerge at different times as the ideal wise counselor or teacher to guide a family member through an important phase. A mentor's role is crucial, but it isn't meant to be a permanent crutch. When the time is right, the mentee steps up to the new challenge.

Grandparents often have a head start on the job. They are eager to spend time with their grandchildren, and the younger set is inclined to listen. Mentoring between them can be as simple as offering to help with homework. Sharing family stories of earlier times can bring a routine history lesson to life in a new way.

If investing is a favorite topic, talking about companies and how stocks work can build money skills better than just handing over a check on every birthday. Grandkids might be surprised to know that their wise grandparents probably made a few bad calls along the way. There's nothing like the voice of experience.

Elders can continue to be mentors long after the basic lessons are mastered. The value of sound advice has no statute of limitations. Given the twists and turns and unpredictability of today's careers, hearing loving but firm words of counsel is valuable to family members of any age.

With members as willing mentors, exactly how do families put their in-house resources to work? In his book *Strategy for the Wealthy Family*, Mark Haynes Daniell suggests that there are seven things the next generation needs to learn:[4]

1. Foundation of values
2. Knowledge and understanding
3. Experience
4. Communication
5. Purpose and responsibility
6. Love and discipline
7. Trust

Family members are not only the best candidates for providing this wisdom; they are the only ones. No one can pass on the family's values better than those who already believe in them.

A strategic family, with its mission and values clear, goals set, and its principles and policies written, is perfectly poised for its members to pass on knowledge and experience. Love, discipline, and trust are added advantages that the mentor instills in the next generation, and this is a win-win situation for the entire family.

When family members see mentors at work, they know everyone's committed to the family for the long haul. A candid word from a mentor delivered with a kind heart is worth a thousand lectures from someone else. When "we can work things out" is the mentor's credo, trust is earned.

Our millennial generation is ready and eager to learn. Despite growing up with more connectivity than ever, today's generation between the ages of 18 and 33 is more isolated than the preceding one. Social networking platforms encourage quantity over quality where success, self-image, and relationships are concerned.[5] It's all too easy to see life as a picture of happiness, even if the image is false. It takes more than editing one's profile page to make genuine progress.

Research shows that millennials are more stressed than any other generation, including boomers and generations X and Y. Rose Kumar, MD, points to six reasons for the millennials' angst:[6]

1. Financial stress
2. Pressure to become independent
3. Less foundational cohesion due to broken families
4. No consistent role models for commitment and fidelity
5. No substitute for parenting
6. Uninspired and unfocused about career goals

Mentors are Dr. Kumar's answer to these challenges. They're a source of help that's sorely needed. Kids from affluent families aren't immune against these challenges. In fact, depression and anxiety are more likely to develop in children from rich families and are twice as prevalent for those whose parents earn more than $150,000 annually than in the population overall.[7] Kids, like the other members of their family, need more than money to thrive.

If the member of next generation need more advice and support as they make the transition to full independence, family mentors can be ideal resources. What makes the mentoring relationship so well suited to a family is that it's a process of mutual sharing. The mentor and the mentee learn together. And because people have different needs at different times, the natural web of family is a fertile ground for both becoming a wise counselor and finding one.

For example, a mentor shows you the ropes. A mentor can tell you what you need to know or where to find the answers. Since families are complex, it's easy to get off course without a guide. James Hughes describes mentorship in terms of the three kinds of learning it offers. First, mentorship involves data, information, knowledge, and wisdom. Applying that to context of family strategy, the first job of the mentor is to hammer home the family mission and values and then to talk about family goals. *What are we trying to accomplish? How are we doing it? What decisions are being made and how are they working?*

Hughes describes the second phase of mentorship as seeking, listening, exchanging, and integrating. If the first phase was about learning what to do, the second phase is about how to do it. *What's the best behavior at the family meeting? How does candid communication happen? When's the right time and place to contribute? Is everyone integrated well into the family mix?*

Finally, the third and last phase of mentorship is about breaking away, differentiating, and pausing. Then the cycle of listening, learning, and integrating repeats.[8] Armed with knowledge, practiced in process, the mentee assumes his or her place at the table. With his or her authentic voice, the mentee starts giving back. Wisdom has been shared, and the cycle begins anew.

A mentorship model is ideal for delivering family education. Money management is an area where mentorship can be particularly helpful. The Rogers family knew it should teach the next generation about money. In the end, the family learned this was just the first step. There was much more work to do together.

It's All About the Money: NOT!

"I've failed," Jon Rogers declared when he called me late one October afternoon to give me an update on how the family meeting went. "I've been trying to get the rest of my family interested in investments, just like we talked about doing, but it's not working. I need a new plan."

It was just after 4:00 p.m. on October 15, and the members of the Rogers family had just trickled out of the well-appointed conference room of the family office after the quarterly investment meeting. When Jon Rogers sold his investment firm, he began educating his family about money as part of the education program we had designed. He knew it was important that everyone be educated about how the wealth would be managed once everything wasn't tied up in the business anymore. He set about doing this with his usual enthusiasm. And, of course, he was passionate about the topic.

"Tell me a little more," I urged. "What makes you think it's not working?"

"Every quarter we have meetings about the investments. Our three boys attend, along with Cindy and me. The financial advisors review everything in the accounts. They give us tons of information about the portfolios, the various strategies, the performance, and an economic forecast. We give everyone a big book of information that's just filled with all the details."

"They all show up for the meeting, but I can tell it's not something that's catching anyone's interest. So even though we've had all these meetings, I still don't know if they've learned much or even care that much about it. It's a disappointment."

"You're being open and transparent about the family wealth, and you're welcoming interest, just like we talked about. This is great. Maybe there's a different approach we could consider."

"Should we have fewer meetings, more meetings, or go to a different place?" he asked, clearly hoping for a quick fix he could use.

"I'd like to suggest that we think about how to make you more of a mentor and less of a teacher, at least when it comes to your family's investments."

"I'm not sure I know the difference."

"A teacher usually has some information that he or she is trying to pass on to another person. The teacher recites things to the student, and the student tries to take it all in and remember it. The process is usually one-sided, and the student is mostly a listener. Does that sound like what happens in your investment meetings?"

"That's exactly what happens. It's a one-way street. I must not be a very good teacher because no one asks any questions."

"A mentor, on the other hand, is able to engage the student by asking questions that create a dialogue. It's a much deeper, give-and-take relationship where both people are engaged in the process. Though it may sound odd, the mentor also learns from the one who is being mentored."

"Let's think about how you can encourage a different type of conversation. Since they're not interested in the technical aspects of investing, you'll need to try a different tack. Here are a few ideas to discuss. *What are your thoughts about the family's wealth? What are your personal interests and passions? Is there anything you think the family should discuss but hasn't? Do you have any suggestions on how the family can support you better?*"

"It's not that you need to stop having the investment meetings. They serve a purpose. But a family conversation about money can be about more than just what's in the portfolios. That's where your role as a mentor comes in."

Several months later, Jon asked me to stop by. We walked down the street for a casual lunch. "We had a family meeting last night, and it was amazing the things my family members had on their minds that I never imagined. The kids realize that the money is being managed just fine right now. They know I'm watching over things. There's really nothing for them to do, so they just listen politely. As long as I'm here, they feel like there's not much for them to add. They're thinking about a lot of things, but they just don't have the same perspective that I do. That's because I made the money, and they didn't."

"What else came up?" I asked.

"The boys are concerned about their own careers. They've been so quiet in the family meetings that I thought they weren't very motivated. Not so. They're worried about just living off the family money. In the economy of the last few years, it's been hard for them to get traction.

"They're ready to get out on their own. I can't keep protecting them from making their own mistakes. And Cindy would like to go back to work, too. Now that the boys are out of the house, she doesn't have a focus. She's a little scared, too. But like the boys, she's ready to leave the nest. As a matter of fact, I could use a new interest, too." Jon looked away, unsure what to do next.

"This is just another phase, Jon," I responded. "It's good that everyone wants to keep progressing. And it's a chance for you to help each other. We all need someone to talk to when we're stuck."

At the next meeting, everyone shared résumés. They brainstormed ideas. They asked questions. They encouraged each other. The family was a family on the move again.

* * *

Families provide many benefits. They offer love, sympathy, teaching, and learning. Financial resources help. Trusted advice is a gift that money can't buy. Those are always the best kind of benefits.

In business, we've come to expect that everyone must evolve to stay successful. Finding an ally or being one is part of the job. Family members need our advice and guidance too. Sometimes we're giving. Sometimes we're receiving.

Take time to ask. Take time to listen. Be a mentor.

Staying on Track

CHAPTER 10

Financial Sustainability: Working with Your Money, Not against It

Taking care of finances is part of the nuts and bolts of running a business. But a CFO does more than manage the numbers. Making good decisions about money takes discipline and skill to stay on track. Avoiding costly mistakes is critical to a firm's fiscal health. Families need a similar targeted attitude to operate in the black and build wealth.

Understanding the fundamentals of investing involves recognizing the difference between a sensible opportunity and something that is simply too good to be true. In the 1630s, Dutch tulips became such a craze that one bulb was selling for the equivalent of a whole estate before the crash.[1] The hope and euphoria of riding a wave disappeared into disappointment when the bubble burst. Tyco, WorldCom, and Countrywide Financial are examples of companies that made making money seem easier than it was. In those situations fraudulent practices eventually led to failures.

For example, Charles Ponzi ensured that his name would forever be connected with deception by using new investors' money to pay off other investors, pocketing millions along the way. Likewise, Bernie Madoff's recent billion-dollar Ponzi scheme destroyed his family as well as the wealth of many more. Many of those taken in were successful and informed investors and money managers. When people become complacent or use poor financial judgment, they can fall victim to Ponzi schemes.

Taking on too much risk can bring down even savvy financiers. Before declaring bankruptcy in 2008, Lehman Brothers was the fourth-largest investment bank in the United States. This fast-growing firm had climbed from 88th to 37th on the Fortune 500 list as its revenue rose from $19 billion to more than $59 billion between 1999 and 2007.[2] Heavy borrowing took a toll on the company's finances when the market turned, and the financial engineering made the firm vulnerable. With real estate prices dropping quickly, the losses mounted. The fall was fast and hard.

Families can be equally susceptible to becoming overleveraged. At some level, it doesn't matter what you have if you're spending too much. Using debt to finance your standard of living can put that very lifestyle at risk. At the end of the day, it's borrowed money. Avoiding tough financial decisions is living on borrowed time. Eventually time runs out.

Gold Florins Weren't Enough

Even the House of Medici, a prominent banking family, powerful political dynasty, and art patron of the Italian Renaissance did not escape fiscal missteps, and these cost the family great wealth and power. Prudent financial decisions can make or break any family. With a family's people as its most valuable asset, keeping everybody financially productive compounds the interest. If members lose focus, even a family that issues its own gold coins can't be protected from financial catastrophe.

The Medicis were not only big-time bankers. They were also innovators in accounting, using new techniques developed in Italy in the fourteenth century, such as double-entry bookkeeping to track debits and credits. So how could a family with that kind of financial acumen let bad loans run its finances into the ground?

Giovanni de' Medici had built the banking business so successfully that 100,000 florins were on deposit from the papal Curia alone. New branches opened throughout Italy and factories making woolens were built. This was expansion and diversification at work in the fifteenth century. As Florence flourished, so did the family's fortunes.

Later generations didn't fare as well. They cared more about politics and art than about business. The people they put in charge were incompetent and untrustworthy. One bad deal followed another. Mismanagement and dishonest employees destroyed the bank's profits. By the time Giovanni's great-grandson Lorenzo de' Medici died, the bank was almost bankrupt. Bank assets were seized and distributed to creditors. Branches were shuttered, and the Medici Bank was no more.[3]

Though the Medicis were one of the wealthiest families of the time, they ultimately ran into financial troubles. While they wielded political power, produced four popes, and greatly influenced the arts, their banking empire didn't survive. It was a wealth transition failure of the highest order.

* * *

When it comes to money, transparency is indispensable. There must be a thorough and detailed process for handling everything from compensation policies to accounting practices. Keeping expenses low and trust high is a winning combination for preserving wealth.

Healthy businesses are careful about their finances. Healthy families should be, too.

Great companies make sure their financial houses are in order. In *Fortune* magazine's 2014 rankings of the most-admired companies, four out of the top five firms received the highest ranking possible for financial soundness.[4] Such blue-chip companies are held in high regard because they can weather downturns and operate profitably even when economic times are bad. Families need to have their financial safety nets in place to sustain themselves through the inevitable ups and downs that occur in every family.

Big company standards for financial strength also apply on the home front. According to Francois M. De Visscher of the University of Massachusetts Family Business Center, sound financial practices and attention to shareholder value are the most important elements of excellence for family-owned companies.[5] Owners want good dividends. However, they also invest for growth. They plan for tomorrow, not just for today.

"Cash is king," is a familiar saying in business. Warren Buffett counts cash flow at the top of his list of criteria when analyzing investments. It's also what pays the bills. Successful firms make sure they have enough liquidity to operate with an adequate financial cushion. Families, too, should be prepared for the unexpected.

There is no shortage of guides available about how to manage money, and the amount of products and services offered to investors by the financial services industry has never been greater. From 1990 to 2012, the number of mutual funds alone increased from 2,395 to over 7,000.[6] But many families still fail to achieve their financial goals. Success means having a plan and sticking to it. Here are a few tried and true habits that never go out of style.

Step 1. Listen to the elders

Save for a rainy day. A penny saved is a penny earned. The early bird catches the worm. Often it's family members who pass on such pearls of wisdom. Translated into financial lessons, these "intergenerational communications" help build practices that defer gratification, build capital, encourage hard work, and instill a sense of appreciation for what has been earned.

Step 2. Start early

Counting on winning the lottery just isn't a good bet. It's smarter to count on low-risk strategies like earning and saving. Financial advisors recommend having a "long time horizon." What this means is that the earlier you start, the more you can accomplish and accumulate. Later in life, capital will be more important, dividends will be more relevant, and financial security will be more likely.

Step 3: Live within your means

Going into debt to fund living expenses is a road to nowhere. Living beneath one's means makes saving possible. Saving creates capital to invest. The "sage of Omaha," Warren Buffett, practices this habit himself.

Step 4: Invest wisely

Though this is easier said than done, the numbers don't lie. Over 30 years from 1983 to 2013, the Standard & Poor's 500 Index achieved an annual return of 11.1 percent, while investors in equity mutual funds earned only 3.69 percent. For a $10,000 investment, this gap amounted to over $200,000. For the 20 years between 1993 and 2013, investors also fell short, earning just over 5 percent on average each year, while the index earned over 9 percent. This meant a shortfall of over $31,000.[7]

State Street's Center for Applied Research completed a study to try to answer the question, "What does true investment success look like?" According to Suzanne Duncan, Global Head of Research at State Street, people did not have investment success because they were overconfident in their investing ability, unable to focus on their stated long-term goals when distracted by noise in the markets, and had come to distrust their advisors and lose interest in receiving professional help.[8]

Both advisors and investors have work to do.

Setting financial goals and sticking to them sounds like a logical way to deal with money. The growing field of behavioral finance seeks to explain why emotions and psychology cause us to make irrational decisions that take us off course. It's tempting for investors and advisors alike to be swayed by how the markets are performing in the short term. Just as with the other parts of a family plan, successful investing requires a long-term strategy.

Investors face tempting distractions that can cause them to lose focus as well as money. If the financial tactics become disconnected from a family's goals, members will ultimately suffer.

Here are a few dilemmas:

- The allure of large gains is an elusive pursuit. There's always a hot idea that promises a way to get rich quick. More often than not, such efforts prove to be futile. It's better to go for quiet, tried and true, long-term compounding of interest. It may seem boring, but it works. If done well enough, the successful investor can afford to purchase many other exciting things by avoiding foolish schemes.
- Following the crowd can take you right off the cliff. It's tempting to jump onto the bandwagon for a popular new product when everyone else is too. Trendy may be fine for fashion. But it's not always wise for investing.
- Using the wrong map leads to the wrong destination. Many people seem to think the financial markets should cooperate with their own personal economic or political viewpoint. It is hard to be right on those factors and then have the markets cooperate with your opinions. It seems better to know that the market went up 8 percent compounded over the last 200 years, albeit not in a straight line, and plan accordingly.
- Making decisions based on short-term market movements is like a whipsaw. It can be painful both ways. Even the experts can't win at timing the market. Getting distracted by what the market is doing today can cause mistakes tomorrow.
- Don't confuse volatility with risk. If stock of a quality company becomes available at a lower price for a short time, that doesn't mean the company has changed. It could just be on sale. Volatility can be measured, fitting into a tight little number. Risk is the permanent loss of capital. Think back to some of the Internet favorites of yesteryear whose market values were once huge, but now the companies no longer exist.

Here are several remedies a family can look to when the financial environment tests its confidence.

- Lean against the wind. Consider the contrarian's point of view.
- Time is your friend. Investing early gives the money more time to grow through the magic of compound interest.
- Don't be forced to sell. Plan in advance for spending so investments don't have to be sold at inopportune times.
- Go for quality. Invest in the best companies. As Warren Buffett says, "Price is what you pay. Value is what you get."
- Practice patience. Making money wisely takes time. It's not a straight path to profits.[9]

Instead of measuring progress against short-term stock market returns, stay focused on what the money is supposed to be accomplishing. The biggest risk families face is the possibility of lowering their standard of living through poor investment choices. Investors who train themselves to think about where the conventional wisdom could be wrong and act on their own convictions can do better than average. Those who can also stick to a sensible long-term plan will likely do quite well.

There's nothing wrong with investing in the family itself. Sometimes the best proposals come from within.

An Inside Job

I placed the sleek, black Chanel bag at the podium for everyone in to see. When the words "emotional spending" appeared on the screen, the women laughed and the men rolled their eyes. It had become a predictable response at my "Financial Fitness" seminars for millennials. It was part of a program to help families prepare the members of their next generation for the responsibilities of inheriting wealth.

"It's my bad habit," I began, holding the pricy purse high to emphasize the point. "I've learned when it's okay to treat myself and when it's just an impulse that should be ignored. People have different financial instincts. Some of us tend to be spenders, and some tend to be savers. It takes experience to understand our relationship to money and education to learn how to manage it well."

Up on the screen, the slides continued to carry other nuggets gleaned over the years of conversations. *Learn the fundamentals of investing. Don't underestimate the value of work, no matter how much money you have. When working with advisors, ask questions. Understand what you own, what you earn, and what you spend.*

It was always during the question and answer period that the challenges of wealth emerged in concrete terms. Couples with younger children worried about raising entitled kids. Singles with significant others wondered when and how to talk with their potential spouses about their money. Those who had seen their families experience the last financial crisis worried whether the same thing could happen again and jeopardize their own wealth. These are real concerns of the rising generation of heirs.

At the end of the seminar, a young couple stood waiting to catch my attention. The husband had a sport coat slung over his arm, while his wife was busy firing off texts. When the rest of the audience was leaving the room, they stayed behind. I invited them over to chat.

"We wondered if we could speak with you privately about our situation," the husband said. "Our money stuff is a little complicated. When I saw that this event was about money, I decided to come," said John. "This is Cindy, my wife," he said.

John's college had organized the event for its local alumni. College officials recognized that among these young graduates were their major donors of the future. Providing these young people with resources now would build loyalty that would encourage philanthropic support from them later.

The three of us sat together in a small private conference room off to the side of the meeting room where the session was held.

"Tell me what's on your mind," I continued.

"Cindy and I don't have a lot of money now, but my family has resources, and my parents have told me that one day I'll inherit my fair share. I'm confident about my business prospects too, but it's still too early to bank on that. I'd like to talk with them about some financial support now, while we can really use it," John explained.

"It's my situation that's the financial problem," Cindy continued. "I have student loans and credit card debt to pay off. With my nonprofit job, it's going to take a while."

This was a couple with a lot of things going for them. They had the best education money could buy. They had a lot in common, but they had very different financial backgrounds. Cindy's challenge was that it had taken hefty borrowing to complete her education. Then came the nice wedding, which appeared as one line item of credit card debt in Cindy's balance statement.

John chimed in, "I'd like to talk with my parents about helping us out. I'm not sure what they'll think. They like Cindy, but we haven't talked about money that much. It just seems like a practical conversation to have."

The cost itself wasn't insurmountable given John's description of his family's financial assets. But he had been financially independent from his parents since college and had been content to live within his means. There hadn't been any need to rock the boat by talking about money. But with his marriage, things had changed.

It was the family mind-set that would need to be addressed. John's parents had made their own way, worked hard, and been financially successful. They hadn't had any help from anyone, and it seemed as though that was the family expectation. John saw things in a more practical fashion. He wasn't looking for a handout, but he also wasn't intimidated by talking about money.

We mapped out a strategy. The couple prepared a proposal of sorts, including their annual budget and stating the amount needed to eliminate Cindy's debt. They pared their expenses. Entertainment extras would have to wait. John would take a part-time job while he prepared to launch his business. The budget would be tight for a couple of years, but they wanted to show that they were willing to make sacrifices. John hoped his parents would consider providing funds as an investment in the family.

A week later, John called with obvious relief and delight in his voice. "We had a very good discussion," he said. " First, I shared the financial plan Cindy and I had developed. Then we spoke with my parents about our goals and asked them for their advice. It was almost as though they were waiting for us to ask for help. They're going to consult with their advisors about the best way to structure things, whether it's a gift or a loan, that kind of thing."

A few weeks later John's parents asked John and Cindy to join them for a meeting with their advisors. The experts explained how things would be organized, documented, and accounted for. Resources would not be squandered. They'd be recycled. It was a straightforward and productive family meeting about money.

The phrase "wealth and happiness" was not one that John's parents would have coined, but by the end of the meeting they knew what it meant. Using their resources to support responsible family needs made them happy. And that was the purpose of having money.

*   *   *

Accumulating and managing money is challenging. Families who are successful at it generally look for help. The wealthy have sought financial advice since at least the sixth century. In those days a royal family would appoint someone it could rely on to take care of its interests, and this office of the majordomo is the root from which the modern family office grew.

Strictly speaking, a family office is a private company that manages the finances of the family who owns it. The concept is centered on the desire for objective advice. The connection to the old private banks of Europe is no coincidence, either. Families want their privacy.

No name is more closely associated with family offices in the United States than that of John D. Rockefeller. By the late 1880s, he was a billionaire, fueled quite literally by his profits from Standard Oil. In 1882, Rockefeller Family and Associates was launched, and as the family's interests evolved, so did the scope of the office's services. Whether the office managed large sums or funded philanthropic causes, the family's interests always came first.[10]

In the close circles of the very wealthy, families often know one another. This is the case with the Rockefellers and the Rothschilds, the powerhouse financial family that made its fortune in European banking. The two families' connections go back to the 1890s, and when the Rothschilds formalized a partnership with the Rockefellers over a century later, it was an example of two dynasties joining forces. This is financial sustainability at the highest level.

Most of us will never have access to the Rockefeller or Rothschild resources for managing our money, but financial advice has become more mainstream. Between banks, brokerage houses, and independent wealth managers, services have become more available and accessible to families. Even so, when it comes to finding the best financial solutions, the path can still be bewildering.

Getting objective advice has proven to be of lasting interest to families, and a whole profession has grown up around it. In 1915, Los Angeles financial analyst A. M. Clifford first began calling himself an "investment counselor" when one of his wealthy clients asked him to review her $30 million in assets. After that, he became passionate about selling advice, not securities.

Around the same time in Boston, three other young men, Theodore Scudder, Sidney Stevens, and F. Haven Clark recognized this need as well and wrote a business plan based on the same idea. Though phrases such as "unbiased expert advice," "diversified portfolio," and "constant supervision of the account" are often touted today by wealth management professionals, those ideas were visionary back then.[11] The principles of these early professionals set the standards that benefit investors today.

Now the options for how families can manage their money are taking another turn. The latest version falls under the umbrella of "robo-advisor." Technology is making online investment advice available at lower costs and to more potential investors. This allows the "do it yourselfers" to do just that by using tools formerly available only to in-house professionals. This is portfolio management without human intervention.

Ultimately, this trend may take financial advice to where it all began, to the family office. Today's family offices remain so costly that only the ultra-rich can afford them. Providing tax and estate planning, risk management, investment advice, philanthropic guidance, and personal services all under one roof is complex. And expensive.

However, technology may soon change things. According to Hannah Shaw Grove, a consultant to family offices, a robo-advised family office could reduce the confusion as well as the costs of high-quality financial management.[12] As people become more comfortable with using technology in more and more aspects of their lives, managing their money is bound to be on the list of things that can be made easier and cheaper. If what was once only available to the likes of the Rockefellers moves downstream, families will surely benefit.

At the end the day, families are responsible for their own financial destinies. Con artists and too-good-to-be-true proposals will always be waiting in the wings. Technology will give us more and more information at a faster and faster pace. Families still need good thinking to filter out the noise.

Making make wise financial decisions in the face of seemingly endless options requires a steady hand and mind. Developing good financial instincts is invaluable. So is finding the right experts to advise you on how to stick to your plan. When your family and its money are working well together, it's a partnership that keeps the legacy strong.

CHAPTER 11

Family Sustainability: Risk and Resilience

"Hope for the best and plan for the worst" is an oft-quoted maxim. Since things don't always go according to plan, every enterprise must anticipate problems and manage the crises that arise. Companies have entire departments devoted to these tasks; they are called risk management.

Risk is the potential of losing something of value, but this something isn't always money. When family ranks high on the list of what we value most, risk management is an essential piece of a family's strategy.

Thinking about potential threats and failures isn't the most natural focus for family members' energies. It's more exciting to envision a positive future. But just as even the biggest and best companies have learned, something can always go wrong. You have to have your emergency plan ready to deploy.

When a project backfires, the buck stops at the top. Leaders have to explain what happened and ensure that it won't happen again. How companies weather the storm depends on how well prepared they are to repair the damage and move forward. Families face inevitable challenges just as companies do. Anticipating what these challenges could be and how to respond to them should be part of every family's planning.

Risk management is risky itself. Take General Motors, for example. It touted its risk-management program as a competitive advantage, but it didn't take its own strategy seriously enough.

In 2012, prior to the emergence of the faulty engineering processes that caused the ignition switch failures, GM's leadership trumpeted the company as a risk-management model for others. In reality, the very internal processes

GM hailed as the best caused problems of monumental proportions.[1] GM failed itself. Families should examine their own operations to ensure the measures they've put in place are working optimally.

When Tony Hayward became CEO of BP, he claimed that safety was his top priority.[2] Given the company's prior record, there was good reason for his concern. A refinery explosion in 2005, a ruptured pipeline in 2006, and a close call with another platform in 2003 demanded vast improvements in risk management. But when the Deepwater Horizon explosion was investigated, it was clear the corporate risk-management strategy had fallen short.[3]

Problems are inevitable for companies involved in complex endeavors. When catastrophe strikes, a clear explanation is essential in order to explain what happened and how the situation is being remedied. This not only protects a company's reputation, it's the right thing to do and preserves trust.

The environmental consequences of the *Exxon Valdez* oil spill were disastrous, but the company only made things worse by communicating with the arrogance that marked its culture. After the incident Exxon lost market share and dropped from being the largest oil company in the world to the rank of third largest.[4] For firms and families, how they recover from problems is a major part of their strategy.

Risks are always waiting in the wings. Some can be prevented, and others have to be managed. They can't be avoided altogether. First, you have to know what the problems are or what they could be. That allows you to prepare for them. Families that have already been practicing habits of open communication and transparent decision making are better able to manage turbulent times.

For example, Arthur E. Andersen, who founded his accounting firm in 1913, was a champion of high standards in the accounting industry. He believed that an accountant's first duty was to investors. There was no place in his philosophy for fraudulent practices. In 2002, the Andersen firm was convicted of obstruction of justice for shredding documents related to its audit of Enron. While the ruling was later reversed, the damage to the Andersen name was so great that the firm, once renowned for its high standards, was nearly destroyed.[5] Its reputation could not be repaired.

Preventable risks are those that arise from within.[6] These fall into the "we should know better" category. When a company's own employees behave in ways that can damage the enterprise, the situation is unacceptable. In a firm or at home, illegal or unethical actions should be off-limits. The likelihood of loss is simply too great.

In this case, the best defense is a good offense. Underscore the mission. Emphasize the values. Make sure everyone knows the rules. Then hold people accountable. This philosophy works in business, and it works for families.

Risk is part of the cost of doing business. For example, bankers know there's risk involved in loaning money. Managers of a global oil exploration company realize that drilling in the ocean can potentially lead to serious accidents. The management of a technology firm understands vulnerability to cyber attacks. These businesses don't stop doing what makes them successful, but they're acutely aware of potential pitfalls. For a wealthy family, having money brings certain hazards—that goes with the territory.

Then there are things that come out of left field. These are the risks that are beyond our control. Natural disasters and macroeconomic changes can't be managed, but they can be recognized as prospective threats.

Understanding risk and having a plan to deal with it is the job of any company of significance. In today's interconnected world, it's also the job of a successful family. For families too must answer the question, "How much risk are we running?"

* * *

Financial risk can hit from all sides, and not only investment activities bear close scrutiny. A family that manages all of its operations with an eye to what can go wrong isn't paranoid—it is careful.

Consider some of the troubles that can disrupt a family's financial progress:

Health issues: Good health is everyone's most important asset. And it's on people's minds. Age Wave, an education and research organization focusing on issues of aging, found that 73 percent of individuals with high net worth are concerned about a potential shortage of providers that are qualified to care for aging patients. Sixty percent said that the cost of health care is their number one financial concern.[7]

Health emergencies can also become economic problems. An untimely death or disability of a primary income earner can disrupt an otherwise stable financial environment. Medical crises can put an enormous strain on finances as well as emotions. Addictions or other behavioral issues pose a multitude of stresses on the family, and most certainly threaten the health of those affected.

Personal security attacks: As wealth grows, so does risk to personal safety of family members. Inadequate protection from fraud, robbery, and extortion by domestic staff and others working in and around the home is a weakness in a family's operations that can prove harmful. Personal details and information shared online can lead to theft by individuals adept at using private information for criminal purposes.

Even reputable organizations can have weak privacy policies. Providing personal information, such as social security numbers, is not always as benign a practice as it may have once been. Inoperable security systems at home and poor emergency planning expose the family to unnecessary risk from "operator error."

Legal and liability risk: Wealthy families are concerned about being targets of lawsuits. However, many are not as well prepared for such an event as they could be. In a study conducted with wealthy families by ACE Private Risk Services, more than 20 percent of the participants said they had no liability insurance policy at all. Often liabilities are underestimated, especially given the amount of assets that could be at risk. Lawsuits resulting from disgruntled former household employees, accidents, character defamation, or slander are the most common.[8]

What's a family to do?

Take advice from businesses that have risk management down to a science. When assessing where to focus your time, energy, and money spent on reducing risks, ask yourself three questions:

1. What could go wrong?
2. Can better planning help the family sustain a shock to the system?
3. Are there any mistakes that family members might make that more training could prevent?

When developing an action plan for managing risk, keep the following things in mind:

- Work to prevent problems that can be controlled.
- Recognize what problems cannot be prevented.
- React promptly to limit any damage.
- Set aside resources to help the family recover from problems that occur.

Here are some ideas to consider:

Health

- Make sure you have designated a medical advocate who can help the family navigate the health care system.

- If there are known health conditions that may damage the family's financial circumstances, incorporate this information into your financial plans.

Personal security and privacy:

- Do background checks on the individuals you hire.
- Someone in the family should know how to access your financial information in case it is erased from computer accounts.
- Set guidelines for the entire family about what private information may be shared with others, especially online. This is especially important for children, who may be more likely to use social media and provide personal details. Monitoring services are available to alert you to cyber problems.
- Don't give out your social security numbers unless it is absolutely necessary.
- Make sure your home security systems are working properly and that everyone knows how to use them.
- Develop an emergency plan for your family and practice it annually.[9]

Legal liability:

- Consult with professionals about the type and amounts of insurance coverage that is prudent given your circumstances.
- If you're on charitable boards, check with them about what their policies provide and include this item on your list for assessment.

Any shock to the system takes its financial toll. When something goes wrong, there's always a price to be paid. Sometimes there's an outright expense, and sometimes it's a blow to future earnings. First comes the cost to fix the problem. Then there may be fines to pay. Finally, there's the time and money spent regaining lost credibility. All these expenditures divert resources away from productive activity.

As worrisome as these costs can be, it's possible to anticipate and plan for some of them. No one escapes the aging process completely unscathed, but health care coverage provides a buffer. Though the checklist of things to do to stay safe and secure keeps getting longer, there are tangible protections to put into place. Risk professionals can design insurance plans to provide some peace of mind.

There's another kind of risk that's more difficult to control: family dynamics. Research shows that disagreements over money are among the biggest factors when couples decide to divorce. Then there's divorce itself—in addition to carrying a high emotional cost—it can be financially disastrous for the preservation of long-term family wealth. While there is no ideal remedy for the economic costs of divorce, a prenuptial agreement is part of some wealthy families' risk-management strategy.

A prenuptial agreement is a contract between two people who are about to wed that spells out how assets will be distributed in the event of divorce or death.[10] These arrangements have garnered attention in the case of high-profile couples, but they have been used in some form for centuries.

Henry S. Gornbein, a family law attorney, offers some advice on how to approach the prenup process. His first caution is to have an attorney represent you who is experienced in family law and in drafting pre- and postnuptial agreements. In addition, he offers these recommendations:

- Make sure the agreement is discussed months in advance of the wedding and not presented at the last minute.
- Be prepared to negotiate and be fair.
- Have provisions so that as situations change, the agreement can be reviewed and revised or else there can be a sunset clause in the agreement.
- Some agreements provide for a sharing of premarital assets after a number of years and a guarantee of spousal support under certain conditions.
- Be fair. Don't be greedy.[11]

Bouncing Back

Fights over inheritances bring out the worst in family dynamics and represent a sad outcome for any family. They pose the biggest wealth-transition risk there is. While there's no foolproof way to prevent future squabbles over money, those who bring some business thinking to the family strategy have a better shot at beating the odds. To quote Benjamin Franklin, "an ounce of prevention is worth a pound of cure."

Every person and every family faces adversity. But some problems simply cannot be predicted or prevented. Experts from a number of fields, including psychology, education, engineering, hazard management, ecology, and social justice are promoting resiliency as a key ingredient that allows us to adapt and move forward.

Resilience is the process of adapting well in the face of adversity, trauma, tragedy, threats, or significant sources of stress. It means bouncing back from difficult experiences.[12] The field of education is embracing resiliency as one of the keys to doing well in school. Author and speaker Paul Tough argues that the ability to cope with adversity is an important component of building something he calls "grit." He believes that along with curiosity, conscientiousness, and self-control, skills for coping with adversity are as important to success as cognitive skills.[13]

In advocating resiliency as worthy of significant philanthropic support, Judith Rodin, president of the Rockefeller Foundation, suggests, "not every disruption has to become a disaster." She has started a grant-making effort to help communities build resilience. She explains that the resilience "dividend" can be seen "when communities become more skillful at managing and preparing for bad times, and because of the changes they've made, are able to reap benefits even when times are calm."[14]

Dr. Rodin presents five characteristics of resilience that organizations should consider:

1. Know your strengths, assets, liabilities, and vulnerabilities and be willing to assess them frequently and to take in new information.
2. Cultivate a diverse range of ideas, information, technical elements, and people.
3. Make collaboration and coordination key parts of your system.
4. Find ways to "fail safely" and prevent one disruption from setting off a chain reaction.
5. Adapt and be flexible in adjusting to changing circumstances.[15]

In this context, a family and community have similar opportunities and challenges. Both need to develop resilience in order to overcome difficult circumstances. At the same time, each offers its members an ideal environment in which to learn resiliency in an atmosphere of mutual support.

- A family that works together consistently on its strategy develops resilience all along.
- When a family defines its mission and values, strengths and assets are clarified.
- As it forms the habit of regular family meetings with substantive and educational agendas, a family absorbs a diverse range of ideas and information.

- When a family practices open and candid communication, members can accomplish a great deal as they collaborate.
- When family members are mentors, they provide a safe place to build skills and confidence. They understand one another's strengths and weaknesses and provide support and additional resources when necessary.

A dynamic family is an ideal laboratory in which to teach and learn resilience. As members evolve and grow, they build greater capacity to solve tough problems and make complex decisions, both individually and together. The benefits accrue to the family.

The topics that land on the family agenda are varied and interconnected and range from how to pass on values to how to pass on money. In every case, a great deal is at stake. Over time, families that keep at it become more resilient, generation after generation.

Long-Term Planning

CHAPTER 12

Family Dividends: Gratitude and Legacy

In most businesses management believes that giving back pays off. Business leaders appreciate that connecting with the community is connecting with customers and is about more than a tax break. Giving back generates goodwill, and it's good business.

Corporate philanthropy is on the rise. According to an in-depth analysis of the trends in giving by 240 leading companies, 59 percent increased their overall giving from 2007 to 2012. In aggregate, the total amount contributed to charity increased by 42 percent.[1] This group includes 60 of the top 100 Fortune 500 companies. For these firms, improving society goes hand in hand with good performance as a measure of business excellence. Families can set the same expectation.

Leaders understand that charitable giving requires personal commitment from the top in order to be effective. In 1999 actor Paul Newman, along with business chiefs John Whitehead and Peter Malkin, formed a coalition of company executives to encourage corporate philanthropy at the highest level. Today, this group includes over 150 CEOs whose firms give over $19 billion annually.

Newman led the way by directing 100 percent of the profits from his food company to charity. He said his greatest reward was to "take what I've got and spread it around."[2] Newman defined his legacy as both performer *and* humanitarian. For him, doing "good work" also meant doing "good works."

Giving is going global, too. Of Fortune 500 companies that make charitable gifts internationally, 81 percent either maintained or increased contributions in 2013, and 86 percent plan to continue to do so.[3] As businesses expand their reach, they also recognize the need to respond to the needs of the local communities where they operate. Contributions are increasingly directed to solve society's problems that also impact the company's future strategy. As mission and values go, so goes the giving. Families can also fulfill their missions and values with philanthropy.

Entrepreneurs are well represented in the ranks of the charitable. According to a 2010 study by Fidelity's Charitable Gift Fund and Ernst & Young, nine in ten entrepreneurs donate to charity. They give personally as well as through their companies, and most donate time as well as money.[4] Those who have what it takes to start from scratch in business also like to give back. They've discovered that it feels good when money goes both ways.

When it comes to philanthropy, what works at the office can also work at home. If family leaders set the example, other members will jump on board. When charity helps the community, everyone lives in a better place.

Doing Well and Doing Good

Big-time billionaires have been increasingly visible on the philanthropy stage since 2010, when Warren Buffett and Bill Gates announced a campaign to encourage the world's wealthiest people to give their money to charitable causes. Younger donors also joined the scene in recent years, with technology stars such as Mark Zuckerberg and Sergey Brin hitting the top of donor lists. Giving back is in vogue.

Some studies now present scientific evidence that giving is good for you. In a 2006 study by the National Institutes of Health, researchers examined the MRIs of subjects who gave to charities. They found that giving stimulates the mesolimbic pathway, the reward center in the brain, and leads to the release of endorphins, which creates the feeling of "helper's high."[5] Neuroscientist Paul Zak links the ability to have empathy for others to the release of oxytocin in our brains.[6] Being kind to others feels good.

Sara Blakely would likely agree with these assertions. She is a successful entrepreneur whose desire to help women inspires her business, Spanx, as well as her philanthropy. In the giving pledge she made when she signed on to Buffett's challenge, Sara talks about how grateful she is for the opportunities she has had to follow her dreams. This entrepreneur lives by the old adage, "what goes around comes around." Sara measures her ultimate impact by what she gives as well as by what she gets.

Giving is part of the culture at Spanx. It's not just the executive office that makes the decisions about how the company will spend its money. Employees run the philanthropy board, research potential grantees, and deliver checks to organizations the company supports. Sara shares more than company profits. She shares the spirit of giving. This kind of inclusive participation is a model families can use as well.

Similarly, Danone, the French yogurt company, and the microcredit institution Grameen Bank, started Grameen Danone Foods in 2006 to produce and provide affordable dairy products for the poor of Bangladesh. This project aims to fight poverty by reducing malnutrition. Its socially responsible mission is part business, part philanthropy.

Inspired individuals from all corners are translating work passions into philanthropy projects. The *Iron Chef America* star Mario Batali uses his love for food to help feed needy children. Professional skateboarder Tony Hawk builds public parks in low-income communities. Craigslist founder Craig Newmark uses his technology skills and the Internet to connect people and organizations that are working for the common good.[7] Families can extend their reach in the same manner.

The 2014 US Trust Study of High Net Worth Philanthropy, conducted in partnership with the Indiana University Lilly Family School of Philanthropy, reports that 98 percent of high net worth households made donations in 2013—the highest rate since the study began in 2006.[8] The two most widely used charitable vehicles used by families, private foundations and funds advised by the donors, hold over $500 billion in assets.[9] Collectively, this wealth can have a tremendous impact, both on those who are receiving and on those who are giving. Linking the two together is the role of philanthropy.

Family philanthropy can be thought of as a new family business, but it's also different. In business the CEO runs the show. In philanthropy, family members often make charitable giving decisions jointly. In a business family values are influential. In philanthropy values are fundamental. Business priorities are driven by profits. Charitable priorities are driven by people.

Big benefits await the family that gives together. Every time the family makes a contribution, it makes a commitment to the family's values and brings its mission alive. As the family supports its values, it builds its legacy. When the family discusses and decides, it collaborates. Overseeing the financial assets trains members to be good stewards of wealth. Working together as partners builds family cohesion.

Members of the next generation receive added perks when they join the family in philanthropy decisions. Financial skills are honed through firsthand exposure to investment strategies and operating budgets. Research skills are sharpened as charitable organizations are evaluated for potential grants. As younger members become knowledgeable about important societal issues, their own perspective is broadened. Instilling a sense of duty and appreciation for the work of past generations promotes family harmony. The name of the game is gratitude, not entitlement.

Generosity offers its own rewards to families that practice it.

Everyday Acts of Kindness

Charity begins at home. Most young people say they learned about the importance of being generous from their grandparents or parents. Growing up in an environment where giving back is the norm makes a difference in the next generation's habits.

Legendary business leaders, such as Andrew Carnegie and John D. Rockefeller, started giving early. At age 33, Carnegie decided that anything beyond the $50,000 per year that he was earning at the time would be given to "benevolent purposes." Rockefeller started even earlier, influenced by his frugal mother, who encouraged the children to add to the weekly church collection plate. He kept track of every expense and gave 6 percent to charity, even in his first-year job as a clerk. Family examples stuck with him.

Other big names from this gilded age of American philanthropy didn't wait until they were millionaires to start giving. By age 32, J. P. Morgan was already a generous donor to important New York cultural organizations, such as the Metropolitan Museum of Art and the American Museum of Natural History. Likewise, George Eastman, the founder of Eastman Kodak, who ultimately contributed over $20 million to MIT, began donating before his eighteenth birthday. Similarly, Julius Rosenwald made small but regular contributions to Jewish causes even as he struggled to support his growing family. First and foremost, these philanthropists cared about other people.

Some of America's most influential families have spent billions from family fortunes to create philanthropic empires. The heirs of Andrew Mellon turned away from business to become major benefactors of the arts and education. Benjamin Franklin's charitable reach was broad and deep. He started a library, a fire department, and the academy that became the University of Pennsylvania. The nation's first hospital was a Franklin-funded venture as well. The matching grant, now an established tool of grant making, was Franklin's idea.[10]

When Howard Hughes took the family reins at age 19 after his parents had died, he already had a philanthropic mission. Today, the Howard Hughes Medical Institute has a formidable presence in scientific and medical research. Similarly, the Julliard School, the highly regarded music school, was founded through the bequest of Augustus Julliard, who had no heirs, and J. Paul Getty's estate created the world's wealthiest art institution. Exceptional institutions now at the pinnacle of their fields began with one person's foresight.

Philanthropy can also be accomplished through a quiet approach. When my client Louisa invited me to join her for tea one winter afternoon, I saw firsthand that she found joy in giving. Being generous made her happy.

Louisa and I entered the hospital's crowded lobby at 4 p.m. sharp. She was always on time for her appointments, because to her promptness showed consideration for others. She was impeccably dressed, exuding a certain formality but also gracious warmth. Sister Julia, an elderly nun, greeted us warmly and escorted us to basement cafeteria where we sat together at a small table for tea.

"Thank you for meeting us, Sister Julia," Louisa said cheerfully, as she gently squeezed the hand of her late mother's high-school friend. "It's so wonderful to meet you. My mother always talked about you and your work with such admiration," said Louisa as she focused her attention on Sister Julia. "Your dedication to serving others inspired her, and your friendship meant the world to her. Now that I've taken on the family's philanthropy activities, I'm so pleased to get to know you myself. I'm also happy for you to meet my colleague Linda, who helps me with some of our family projects now since Mom has passed on."

"Your mother and I always stayed in touch through the years. We laughed, we cried, we reminisced. We were best friends," Julia said with a gentle voice. "Every year she sent a donation to support the hospital. She never forgot me."

Louisa continued her inquiries with empathy and admiration for Julia's life of service. After college, she became a nun, devoting nearly sixty years to caring for the poor and sick. She guided us on a tour of the hospital, explaining with ardent passion her devotion to her vocation as a nurse.

"This has been a wonderful afternoon," Louisa said to Julia as we finished our tour. "You'll be hearing from us."

Louisa's family had been wealthy for generations. Her parents were generous, and wanted their daughter to be prepared to run the family's private foundation some day. Louisa was exposed to the ins and outs of family and money early on. She was told the family stories, hearing firsthand how hard it was for her ancestors to earn their wealth and keep it. She was taught a sense of duty. When the older generation passed on, she was prepared.

Louisa and I met the following week to talk about the grants her foundation was considering. As we were organizing the files of proposals, I asked her about how she became engaged in philanthropy.

"My family involved me early on in the discussions. I learned what our mission statement meant by seeing it in action. I watched how money was put to work to accomplish something specific. When I began making decisions, I started small so that I could understand the impact of my gift. Over time, I grew into bigger things." Louisa paused thoughtfully. "Sister Julia was always kind to my mother. After their years of devoted friendship, I know Mother would want to continue to support her work. It helps others and so does she."

Louisa received good coaching on the business side of philanthropy, and it was clear she was applying those skills to good ends. But she had also learned something else from her family: it was good to be kind.

"Louisa, you've always focused on sticking to your mission, having a strategy for your giving, and understanding the finances involved. You had a head start on all this. Is there anything else you think is important?"

"Happiness. Giving makes families happier. That's the magic ingredient for successful philanthropy. "

*　*　*

Giving to charity sounds like the right thing to do. Lots of people must agree. Nearly $300 billion was contributed in 2011 by Americans alone.[11] There's no shortage of needs in the world. For families of good fortune and good will, money and good intentions are available as well. Many families have the potential to become involved. They just need a model to follow that can be scaled to their particular experience and capacity.

A philanthropy plan is much like an exercise regimen or a healthy diet. We need to keep at it to make it effective. It needs to be tailored to our particular preferences. As donors, we need to feel successful along the way, or we won't stick with it. But to be successful, we have to work at giving just as we do other endeavors that are important to us..

You don't have to be Warren Buffett or Bill Gates to make an impact. The average donor-advised fund holds about $225,000, and many private foundations are valued under $1 million. Just like many family businesses, charitable funds often start small and grow over time. To continue for generations requires a consistent commitment by the family.

Just like rest of the family's efforts, philanthropy needs a plan. Here are the steps that I have found important to consider at the outset. Charitable giving can be enormously meaningful for the family. Just like any other endeavor, it takes time to establish.

1. **Set a mission**: Decide what you would like to accomplish and what the aspirations of the effort are likely to be. Let the family mission statement and values guide the focus for giving. When charitable projects are in sync with the family's purpose and principles, members are more engaged. My family survey includes basic philanthropy questions that can start the conversation.

2. **Define decision making:** Set up a governance structure and educate family members on giving procedures. Decide who will coordinate the effort. Determine how decisions regarding charitable gifts get made and who will make them. Consider if and when members of the next generation and spouses have the opportunity to participate. Whether you set up a donor-advised fund, a private foundation, or an annual check-writing plan, seek outside advice on the legal requirements of the vehicles before choosing a vehicle.

3. **Align with other financial goals:** Consult with your financial and tax advisors to determine the amount of funds that are prudent to allocate to philanthropy as well as which assets to donate. It may seem obvious, but it's important remember that once the funds are contributed (to a donor-advised fund or private foundation), they are no longer available for the family's use.

4. **Establish a charitable budget:** Determine the scope of your grants: how much, how many, how often. The amount of money that will be available for donations influences the projects that you can fund. From a few thousand dollars to millions, there are many worthy causes that will benefit greatly from your family's efforts. Matching the money to the scope of the work makes it more effective.

5. **Select grantees:** Research the issues and landscape in your area of focus. Complete due diligence on potential grantees. With a clear mission in hand, learn about organizations that are most suited to your interests and philanthropic budget. Many families include site visits to potential

grantees as part of the due diligence. This is valuable for the family as well.

6. **Evaluate:** Ask for feedback from the charities in order to assess what your giving accomplishes. Even the most experienced philanthropists have to work at understanding the effectiveness of their gifts. Set the expectation of communication between you and your grantees. Establishing a dialogue leads to better relationships and results.

7. **Adapt and grow:** Philanthropy is a dynamic endeavor. Be open to adjusting your plans and evolving your strategy as you learn. As new family members become involved, welcoming their input is essential if you want to hold their interest. Just as businesses are on the lookout for new opportunities, effective philanthropy should respond to changing times, both in the family and in society.

8. **Plan for the future:** Develop your succession plan. Think ahead about how long the family's philanthropic endeavors will continue. Some funds are set up for perpetuity, while others are structured to continue for a specific period of time. If the younger generation is expected to manage the family's philanthropic efforts, consider the time and talents available for this purpose.

Charitable activity can be the linchpin that ties the rest of the family plan together. It creates a fresh avenue for communication and education with family members of all ages. In making decisions about how to use their private money for the public good, members share passions, make decisions together, and get on-the-job training on finance and wealth stewardship. It puts theory into practice.

Millennials are putting their own stamp on philanthropy. According to the 2014 Millennial Impact Report by consultant Achieve, 87 percent of those between the ages of 20 and 35 gave a financial gift to charity in 2013.[12] These young people may be called the "me" generation, but they also put their money where their mouth is. They want to make the world a better place.

As the most connected generation in history, multitasking millennials want to engage in business and philanthropy at the same time. Over half of those interviewed say they would take a pay cut for a job that changes the world for the better. According to a 2012 study, 93 percent would buy a product because of its association with a cause. By 2020 this age group will make up over half the work force. There's power in numbers.[13]

The same technology that connects people to each other affects how they do philanthropy. From doing money transfers to microfinancing, mobile phones and social media allow instant action. Leading the charge with her efforts to expand giving through technology is Laura Arrillaga-Andreessen, a Silicon Valley millionaire who advises technology entrepreneurs on how to give. Through her foundation, she's providing online resources to take philanthropy to the masses.

Arrillaga-Andreessen brought philanthropy to academia over a decade ago when she started teaching at the Stanford Graduate School of Business. Her MOOC (massive open online course) version is a six-week online course. She predicts that technology will continue to impact philanthropy as millennials collaborate to create change.

Her personal story is a prime example of one generation learning from another and moving forward. Inspired by her late mother's lifelong work with nonprofits, Arrillaga-Andreessen came to appreciate the power of the experience of helping others when she cared for her terminally ill mother. Now she's continuing that legacy. She's just doing it on her own terms.

There's no right or wrong way for a family to chart its course on philanthropy.

The "why" is much more important than the "how." Strategies and tactics may evolve from one generation to the next. Even the most experienced philanthropists are always adapting their approaches as they learn. As long as family members continue to tap into a spirit of gratitude, good things will be accomplished.

Beyond Family: The Power of Legacy

Most of us want to be remembered fondly by family and friends. Being generous certainly is part of that picture. Philanthropy can make one's footprint in the world much larger. Our potential for impact is far beyond what the dollars alone will buy.

The first philanthropist who impacted me was Annie Lowe Stiles. She was born in 1884 in Campti, Louisiana, as one of twelve children. When her father died in 1900, Annie and her brother Rufus helped their mother hold the family together. Four years after her father's death, Annie married

William Pierce Stiles, a native of Waxahachie, Texas. It was a tough beginning, but things would soon change.

Mr. Stiles became interested in the oil business, and he turned out to be good at it. He founded the Town of Trees, Louisiana, and made it the center of his operations. His commercial interests prospered, and the couple started giving back. After William died in 1932, Annie ran the business and the philanthropy.

Annie's brainstorm was called Camp Stiles, "A Roving Camp for Boys." She founded it on the principle that "The Youth of Today are the Leaders of Tomorrow." The camp was established on the theory of learning by doing, and it offered outdoor activities and travel. These educational trips extended to 45 states and six foreign countries, giving the kids experiences they never could have dreamed of. The goal was to encourage self-reliance, endurance, and positive self-esteem.

The community still benefits from Annie's philanthropy. She made sure that it would continue. The local foundation administers the Stiles fund, and Annie's story still inspires others. Though Annie had no children or grandchildren to take over the family philanthropy, the ideals and causes continue. Annie's legacy lives on.

The Stiles family succeeded in business, but the couple's philanthropy has made an even larger impact. When Annie and William began supporting local causes in the 1920s, nobody could have predicted the future of the family. Through tragic events, the family itself ceased to exist. The wealth could have disappeared too. Annie Stiles didn't let that happen.

She invested her time, talents, and treasure for long-term impact. She made her mission and values clear. She passed on her wealth for the benefit of others. She made a difference.

* * *

Only a few will have the resources to become household names in the world of philanthropy. Most will never be known around the world for diseases cured or billions given. But many have the opportunity to help their communities and in doing so inspire others to follow.

The stories of personal generosity inspire others to act. It starts with simple acts of kindness.

The ancient Greeks viewed philanthropy, which literally means "love of humanity," as the essence of civilization. Plato may be best known as a great philosopher of antiquity, but he was also an early family philanthropist. He left his farm to a nephew with instructions to use the proceeds to support students and faculty at the academy Plato had founded. Though twenty-first-century philanthropy seems chic, using wealth to pass on values and help others isn't a new idea. It also hasn't gone out of style.

CHAPTER 13

Family R&D: Preparing the Next Generation

I n business, meeting the needs of tomorrow's customers requires constant innovation. Staying ahead of the game *is* the game. Success isn't simply about churning out the next product first. Achieving the right balance between sticking with the status quo versus trying something new is every company's challenge. This also applies to families as they strive to preserve their legacy while evolving with changing times.

Research and development is a staple of corporate growth strategies. In 2014, $1.6 trillion was targeted for research globally with the United States alone accounting for $465 billion of that amount. Research drives innovation. According to Battelle, the world's largest nonprofit research and development organization, historical evidence shows that innovation contributes to increased competitiveness for solving society's greatest challenges in health, energy, and security.[1] Families that instill a sense of curiosity as well as a spirit of lifelong learning among their members are prepared to meet challenges as they come.

By using their smarts to seize opportunities, businesses and families can create new wealth. By the same token, missed opportunities and stiff competition can destroy good fortune—for a family just as well as for a firm. "Eating the seed corn" stunts growth and hurts prosperity. Guarding it carefully provides for the future.

Entrepreneurs know that risk of failure is constant. They also understand that "safe and stable" is only a short-term strategy. As the pace of change accelerates, businesses and families alike must be alert to forces, both external and internal, that lead to gradual decline. Capital must be constantly replenished. Stories about vast sums being squandered are legendary. Unfortunately, many times they are true. Unrealistic goals and big spending can bring succeeding generations up short.

For example, Huntington Hartford, heir to the A&P grocery store chain, lost millions through failed opportunities and a lavish lifestyle. In 1940, the Hartfords were ranked among the country's richest families, but by 2004 Hartford had declared bankruptcy and moved to the Bahamas. Peter Pulitzer was the grandson of publishing magnate Joseph Pulitzer, but he ultimately had to be bailed out financially by his ex-wife's husband. Bernhard Stroh founded his beer company from scratch in 1850, and by 1980 the Strohs had a $700 million family fortune. By 2000, the company had been taken over and broken up.[2]

The key to avoiding such experiences lies in recognizing that even the most substantial companies and families are prone to stagnation. "Too big to fail" no longer applies. Agility and creativity stave off apathy and prevent decline. In a study of thousands of firms, *Fast Company* magazine describes a number of factors that characterize successful innovators. They can be summed up as follows:[3]

- Strong execution counts.
  The smartest companies focus on doing a few things very well.
- Consistent investment in innovation is important, even though the payoff ebbs and flows over time.
  The best companies are always working on new ideas.
- At the end of the day, businesses have to make money.
  Good businesses are financially self-sustaining.
- Sustainability strategies are a given for today's companies.
  "Green" is not a fad. Savvy companies incorporate environmentally sound practices into their business models.
- Global talent is an asset.
  New opportunities can be uncovered by incorporating a broad reach.
- Passion matters.
  Forward-thinking companies understand that people are more productive when they are doing what they love.
- Don't get bogged down by bureaucracy.
  Sluggishness slows progress. Progressive companies keep things moving.
- Stay focused on keeping customers.
  Don't lose sight of who made you successful in the first place.

- Use technology software to advance.
  Innovative companies know they will be outpaced without it.
- Dream big.
  Thriving companies are ambitious.

While these characteristics describe the spirit of innovation in twenty-first-century language, these very concepts have worked for generations. Entrepreneurs who get it right can create lasting benefits for their customers and their families. One stunning example is sometimes known as the "first family of pepper sauce." [4]

An Island of Opportunity

Avery Island, off the coast of Louisiana, is home to a story seasoned with sugar, salt, and spice. It's also home to a story of families that have executed their strategy well. The roots of business on the island are found in the sugarcane grown there by John Marsh in the early nineteenth century. It was a commercial venture that fit well with the times.

The Avery family came on the scene when Marsh's son-in-law, Daniel Dudley Avery, married Sarah Marsh and joined the sugar business. He stayed in the family firm, but in due course he was forced to diversify. Fortunately, he had already been pursuing another avenue. He found it in the island's salt dome.

The area was rich in salt deposits, and Avery's salt mine produced millions of pounds of this necessary staple for the Confederacy during the Civil War. Though the sugar plantation was destroyed during the conflict, the salt business thrived. Salt is still mined today by the Cargill Company. The Averys recognized the need for outside help to expand their reach. Their innovative spirit didn't stop there.

Edmund McIlhenny had married Mary Avery, but when his career as a banker was derailed by the war, he literally had to sow new seeds. A food lover and avid gardener, he returned to the island to find that his beloved pepper plants had survived and thrived. He used them to create a spicy sauce to enliven the bland diet of the Reconstruction South. McIlhenny's pepper mash experiment is a perfect example of using family R&D to help launch a new enterprise.

He patented the formula and labeled it "Tabasco," a word of Mexican Indian origin believed to mean "place where the soil is humid."[5] From his 1868 crop of peppers and 658 bottles of sauce, Tabasco has grown to become a household name. Today McIlhenny's great-great-great-grandson Anthony

McIlhenny Simmons runs the company. The seeds are still planted in green-houses on Avery Island. Though the business has operations all over the world, the family has not forgotten where the business started.

McIlhenny has turned its brand into a global leader. The labels are printed in 22 different languages and are shipped to more than 165 nations. It has hundreds of co-branded products. Tabasco sauce is a staple on restaurant tables around the world. This is a family and a business that continues to demonstrate its staying power. It sticks to its mission, but it doesn't get stagnant.

In addition to preserving the family legacy, the McIlhennys also sustain their community. E. A. McIlhenny, the son of the inventor, became an avid hunter and naturalist, publishing scholarly articles on wildlife and conservation. He had a passion for Louisiana's birds and built a small pond on the island to encourage them to nest there. Tens of thousands of egrets and herons still return to "Bird City" every spring and summer. This McIlhenny took his talents in a different direction, but he became no less impactful.

Today Avery Island's lush gardens, rookeries, and wildlife areas are open to visitors. Along with its environmentally conscious operational processes, the company has sustainability efforts that go much further. As coastal restoration advocates, the McIlhennys work to protect the culture that sustains them.

The McIlhennys have been able to survive the "shirtsleeves to shirtsleeves in three generations" threat that has plagued so many families. Their founders set down a clear mission, and succeeding generations continue to execute on it.

From global sales to expanded products, this family has developed a good idea into a broader platform for success. With many employees still living on the small island where it all started, loyalty to the company runs deep. The McIlhenny name is still on the labels. The family has never lost sight of its roots.

There's no question that problems and threats have challenged this family since the 1860s. In the early years, war took its toll on the region. Competitors have produced other good hot sauces. Business has gone global in a world shrunk by communications technology. Company leadership transitions have been necessary as family members have passed on. Forward thinking has allowed the family to thrive.

* * *

All enterprises should incorporate innovation-friendly habits to ensure future success. This is as necessary for families as it is for businesses. Past accomplishments should be respected, but it's novel approaches that drive the future. Here are seven ways—call them the family's R&D strategies—to unleash creative power in a family.

1. *Embrace the family's diversity to expand its opportunities.*
   Members offer a range of skills and talents that can contribute to the family's success. Being open to different perspectives enriches discussions and contributes to better decisions. Everyone has something unique to contribute.

2. *Manage spending for today. Build new wealth for tomorrow.*
   Financial health is a must. This requires sound fiscal habits to be adopted by current generations and new sources of revenue for future generations.

3. *Sustain the world through philanthropy.*
   Leave things in good shape for the next generation. Every family should give back as much as it takes. This increases the chances for success for those that follow.

4. *Operate with a global perspective.*
   Be aware and knowledgeable about the larger world in which the family lives and works. This helps the family to remain competitive in its endeavors.

5. *Stay connected. Technology helps.*
   Use new tools to encourage family members to exchange ideas and communicate. Drifting apart contributes to decline.

6. *Encourage members' passions.*
   Support one another's dreams. Inspire the next generation to be productive.

7. *Have fun together.*
   Family bonds renew the spirit! Optimism encourages the development of new ideas.

Families need to find their own avenues to stimulate fresh approaches to their plans. Experiencing different environments together through travel can breathe new life into a family's thinking. Adventure invigorates the soul as well as the agenda.

People have been intrigued by travel for centuries. For example, Seneca, one of ancient Rome's leading intellectuals, described the benefits this way: "Travel and change of place impart new vigor to the mind."[6] Getting family members away from their normal routines offers a shift in perspective. Leaving old habits behind to try new things paves the way for innovative thinking.

Travel philanthropy can bring provocative thinking into the mix and get members out into the world and in touch with humanity. They begin to view issues through a new lens. Travel philanthropy is also a way to give back that's "up close and personal," whether through a trip for hands-on community service in a different culture or through a journey to see how a charitable investment the family has made is impacting the world. Even disaster zones aren't off limits to volunteers who want to be on the ground and working.

These are not your garden-variety vacations. This is travel that makes a difference, for the world and for the family. This is travel designed to challenge conventional ways of thinking. It stretches the mind while strengthening the bonds among the family members. This type of travel is a bridge to humanity, and that's good for the family's heart.

A safari to East Africa takes on a different tone when it includes several days of work at projects that focus on water issues. A journey to Thailand brings three generations together in a new way when they donate time and effort to protect Asian elephants in the wild. When family members see first-hand the contributions that elephants have made to the survival of the family, they understand why the elephants are always fed first.

Shared experiences, setting aside time away from the routine of work, all provide ways for families to bring different experiences to their own growth and development.

*   *   *

If research fuels innovation, it's the successful implementation of a new initiative that brings value to the enterprise. Even groundbreaking ideas don't get anywhere unless they are executed skillfully. For a conglomerate as for a household, ultimate success depends on capable leadership.

Organizations of all kinds dedicate considerable amounts of time and money to improve the capabilities of managers. In total, US companies spend almost $14 billion annually on leadership development.[7] Colleges and universities offer many degree programs on leadership, and business schools provide a varied array of customized options. No matter where one stands on the question of whether great leaders are "born" or "made," leadership has become big business.

Families face an inevitable need for new leadership. Whether they own and operate firms or are primarily concerned with preservation of wealth and legacy, their next generation will need to be prepared to assume greater responsibility. Those who have fostered an environment of sound governance and open communication are already well prepared to add leadership development to their strategy.

Stephen P. Miller of the Family Business Consulting Group identifies four best practices for leadership development:[8]

1. Ensure that next-generation leaders have job assignments with real responsibility, accountability, and risk either inside or outside the family business interests.
2. Provide accurate feedback on performance, often from trusted non-family leaders in the business.
3. Create a positive and supportive family climate.
4. Start early.

Experience is the best teacher. Work experience is critical for the next generation because it instills an appreciation for what it takes to earn money. If the family owns a firm, its employment policies should be spelled out clearly. It's always critical to get the right person in the right job, and it's especially true with family members in family businesses.

Keeping family businesses in the hands of family leaders has proved to be a tough challenge. The Family Business Institute states that only about 12 percent make it to the third generation. This statistic points out just how rare stories like that of the McIlhenny family are. Along with remaining relevant, the successful firms say that deciding how to hire and promote family employees is a key factor.[9]

Following in Dad's Footsteps

"I have great news! Randy wants to come to work for the restaurants," Alan announced with boisterous enthusiasm during the family's company board meeting. "He'll be finishing college next spring, so the timing is right." The four siblings, who served as the board of directors, were enjoying a scrumptious lunch in one of the private dining rooms of the family's original restaurant in the historic section of their East Coast city. "We've been talking about bringing on the next generation. Randy is passionate about the food business, and he's got the talent for it. He's someone we can train from the ground up. Let's get him on the job."

Alan had been running the family restaurants since his dad retired about a year ago. Along with his dad, Alan, his two brothers, and their sister were board members. I had met Alan through a nonprofit board with which we were both involved. He had asked me to help draft some of the policies for the family's written agreement, and I was attending the board meeting as part of that process.

It was an opportune time for me to interject. "I know you're pleased with Randy's interest, as well you should be. The idea holds great promise for the business, and for Randy. Let's pause for a moment and make sure you've considered everything involved," I suggested.

"What could be better? He's my oldest son," Alan commented. His brother Phil chimed in, "Yeah, I agree." Steve, the other brother, was more cautious. "I'm all for family in the business, but it does set a precedent that we'll need to address as the younger kids come along." Their sister Molly added, with some anxiety in her voice, "I know my daughters will be paying attention to how we handle jobs for their generation."

"Let's use this as an opportunity to think ahead," I suggested. "Your family agreement should include a set of employment policies. Are his responsibilities clear? Does he have the skills and experience to succeed at the job? How will he be compensated? What is his career path? How will his performance be evaluated?"

After some discussion, the board agreed on a general philosophy for family members who wanted to work for the company. They'd have to apply and be qualified for the job just like any other candidate. They'd be eligible for company stock based on good performance. I drafted a set of policies based upon their discussion, and the board approved the policies at its next meeting.

A few weeks later, Randy came to the office for an interview during his college holiday. The board had asked me to meet with him to review the employment policies for family members and talk with him about the opportunities and challenges of working in a family enterprise.

"Randy, it's important with any job you're considering that you learn as much as you can about the responsibilities and expectations in advance.

So now that you've talked with other folks today, and we've reviewed the job description and all the details, do you have any questions or thoughts?" My job was to serve as an outside advisor to bring an objective voice to the discussion.

"Well, it's really cool to think about joining the family business. I've been in and out of our restaurants my whole life. I just love them. It's something that's always been in the back of my mind," Randy's voice trailed off as he glanced at the bustling kitchen activity behind us.

"But after being back here today with this very real opportunity in front of me, I'm thinking that it's too soon for me to come back here to work. I'm going to take another job first. I need to get some hands-on chef's experience outside the family restaurant. One day I hope to come back, but I want to make sure I'm ready."

"Kudos to you, Randy," I congratulated him on his thoughtful assessment.

"Dad may be disappointed, but I want to feel confident that it's the right path, not just the convenient one."

"Your dad will be fine. He'll also be very proud of you for believing in yourself and taking a risk."

Randy had it right. By taking a job outside the family company, he'd learn the ropes from the ground up in a different environment. That way, he'd always know he could make it on his own. He'd also bring new ideas back home when he was ready to return. His career plan was also a leadership development plan.

*   *   *

We all need a safe place to talk about what matters to us. In today's competitive world, next -generation family members should be able to look to their family for encouragement as well as for candid conversations as they chart the course of their careers. Families with an established practice of regular meetings have a head start on fostering leadership for the future. Whether what is needed is a gentle suggestion or time for a serious change in direction, the family should be a source of sound advice.

Honest feedback is essential for us to be the best we can be. Everyone benefits from regular, professional input about performance. This feedback can be a 360-degree review, which is used in many companies, or something less formal; in any case, an assessment of what is going well and what can be improved upon avoids frustration and costly mistakes. If members are working outside a family company, they should be able to count on those inside the family as sounding boards and advisors.

Skills matter. Contacts help. It's rarely ever too early to recognize and develop leadership capabilities. Experience is gained through school and community activities, part-time work, and internships. The family network is a valuable resource, whether it offers informal coaching and support or provides contacts for gaining valuable information about career opportunities. There's nothing wrong with opening doors for family members who are prepared to make the most of opportunities.

Whether in a company or a family, future success is not guaranteed. It must be earned. Growing companies are always on the lookout for new products that will build their brands. While the profits often aren't immediate, they can ultimately have a big impact if the new products are successful.

When family members enhance their talents and leadership skills, this is R&D that pays off down the road. Though there is no surefire path to prosperity, those who keep learning have a distinct advantage. Good teachers encourage learning.

There's no better teacher than family.

CHAPTER 14

The Future of Your Family: No Success without Succession

The clock is always ticking. That's a cold, hard fact that none of us likes to face. For those in positions of influence, this can be especially difficult because it means stepping back from roles and responsibilities that have been embraced with pride and gusto. Future profits depend on future people, and the talent pipelines need to be filled. Passing on a legacy is the ultimate test of success, and it's much more than handing over the office keys.

Companies know that planning for the changes in leadership is crucial; however, it's hard for them to do:

According to a 2010 survey by Korn Ferry, 98 percent of firms believe a CEO succession plan is important, but only 35 percent actually have one in place. Development Dimensions International's 2011 Global Leadership Forecast found that only 1 in 3 organizations have high-quality, effective development plans for leadership in general, and in a 2011 American Management Association Enterprise survey, only half of respondents said their organizations were effective in their ability to retain high-potential employees.[1]

The price for procrastination on succession planning can be high. CEO transitions are generally vulnerable times for companies. Investors are twice as likely to sell shares during a CEO transition than to buy them. All things being equal, nearly 40 percent of investors said they would sell a stock solely on the basis of the company having a new CEO, whereas only 15 percent said they would buy the stock on the same basis.[2] Shareholders vote with their money, and succession planning is no longer something just for boardroom debate. A company's customers also pay close attention.

Changes at the top can sap confidence if they don't go well. The brief tenure of Leo Apotheker as CEO of Hewlett Packard is an example of a transition that put the company's value at risk. He failed to establish a clear direction, and the market reacted negatively to uncertainty about the company's strategy. By the time he was dismissed from the company less than one year after assuming the CEO role, HP's stock had lost more than 45 percent of its value. The costs in lost credibility were equally significant.

Changes at the top don't have to go badly. When the late Steve Jobs resigned as CEO of Apple Inc. for health reasons, the potential for damage to the company was high. But because the firm executed a well-crafted plan, investor confidence remained intact despite Jobs's departure. As passionate as he was about his company, steps were in place to help it prosper without him. Other big firms, such as Disney, General Electric, and Proctor & Gamble, have shown that leadership change can be accomplished successfully.

Preparing well for the future is an art as well as a science. The Stanford Business School and IED's 2014 Report on Senior Executive Succession Planning and Talent Development outlined six key elements of successful succession planning:[3]

1. Strategic planning: Determine what capabilities, roles, and talent are needed to execute the business strategy today and in the future.
2. Talent assessment: Gauge the Executive team's bench strength. Do we have who we need and if not how do we get there?
3. Recruiting: Develop a pipeline for key roles.
4. Performance assessment: Let people know they are valued contributors and provide them opportunities for development.
5. Development: Create development plans for individuals.
6. Retention and engagement: Invest in rewards and recognition. Foster a productive work environment. Offer opportunities for development.

To put this advice to good use, companies have to translate it into their own language. A company's legacy is built around its culture. Much of a firm's future strength lies in the unleashed talent of those who are already contributing to the organization's success. People are capable of stepping up.

They're just waiting to be asked. Similar pitfalls and potential exist for families during transitions, and the stakes are just as high.

Between 2031 and 2045, as much as 10 percent of the total wealth in the United States is expected to change hands every five years.[4] The sons and daughters of the boomer generation will be in the drivers' seats. Preparing for the changing of the guard is something every family needs to do, and this is the final measure of a leader's mettle.

In a family, leadership succession is inevitable. However, it's often completely internal, with even fewer guideposts for progress than companies have. If members have been thinking of their family with a business mindset, they have a big head start on succession planning. They already know that wealth is about a whole lot more than money.

Number one, strategic thinking is already the norm. Everyone understands the mission, and values are intact. The pipeline of family talent is full. The family has also been busy. Whether in a business, favorite philanthropy, or family governance, a spirit of collaboration is in place. Working through thorny issues isn't new to the members. No family is free of foibles, but in an atmosphere of open communication, differences can get worked out. When it's time to face the loss of loved ones, the extra baggage has been left behind.

Famous Feuds

Celebrity status does not guarantee protection from blunders that result in lost fortunes, long fights, or both. Once you're gone, no one can ask you what you intended to have done with your estate. But make no mistake, if disagreements occur over inheritances, such disputes can have devastating consequences for those you leave behind.

For example, Johnson & Johnson is known as a "family company." The estate fight caused by one of the sons of its cofounders put that moniker to the test. When John Seward Johnson died of prostate cancer in 1983, he left most of his fortune to his third wife, Barbara Piasecka, a former maid more than four decades his junior.

John's children contested this outcome, certain their father had suffered abuse by his wife. It took three years and nearly $10 million in legal fees to find that Johnson was not mentally competent when he signed the will. The children were awarded $160 million by the judge.[5]

Doing nothing, leaving things unclear, or putting someone unqualified in charge of your estate can be expensive and painful for heirs. Similar stories about other celebrities abound. For example, singer Jimi Hendrix failed to specify his wishes, and this resulted in a fight that lasted thirty years beyond his death. Olympic athlete Florence Griffith-Joyner's will was lost, and her probate estate took over four years to close. Similarly, actor Marlon Brando made oral promises to his housekeeper, which led to lawsuits after his death.

Doris Duke put her butler in charge of her estate of $1 billion dollars, which led to a bitter court fight when he spent some of the money on himself. Even Princess Diana's wishes weren't carried out as she may have intended because the instructions about her personal belongings weren't part of her will.[6] Clearly, the dotting the i's and crossing the t's is crucial.

Even if you believe such haphazard planning would never happen in your family, no one should underestimate the perils of wealth transition. Money sharpens the edge on every emotion. On the one hand, it provides the greatest opportunity for your successors to demonstrate responsibility and good stewardship. On the other hand, envy and jealousy can be unwelcome interlopers.

* * *

Just as companies take specific steps to get their succession plans in good shape in advance, families should do the same. No family strategy is complete without a succession plan.

- **Develop your philosophy.** Deciding with whom and how you wish to share the wealth it has taken a lifetime to accumulate is a reflection of your unique life choices. It's personal.
- **Inventory everything you own.** Questions about what you wish to leave spouses, children, family, friends, and charities can be complex. Give yourself time to consider the options. And time to change your mind.
- **Document your wishes.** Invest in professional help. Misunderstandings caused by incomplete or poorly drafted legal documents can be costly, both financially and emotionally. Make sure your next of kin or other representative knows where to find the information.
- **Don't forget the "stuff."** Personal possessions are particularly prone to cause problems among heirs, because these represent their most cherished family memories. Consider asking your loved ones in advance which items would be most meaningful to them as you are deciding who will receive what. You may be surprised. The smallest items sometimes have the most meaning.

- **Determine who will manage your estate for you.** And then talk with that person about it. Serving as an executor or trustee is an important responsibility. It's a business matter, not a matter of who's necessarily closest to you. A professional trustee can be a prudent choice.
- **Discuss your plans with your family.** Communicate. Communicate. Communicate. There are different points of view about whether it's wise to talk about dollars. What is more important is explaining why you're doing what you're doing. Everyone may not agree with your decisions, but at least you want your family to understand your rationale. This is a truly the time when "no regrets" matters.
- **Tell your story to those you love.** You're so much more than what you own. Don't you want to pass that wealth on as well? Write a letter. Make a video. Whatever method you choose, take the time to tell others in your own words what's been important to you. Telling your story is as good for you as it will be for them.

Blood, Sweat, and Tears

"Joe and I are ready now," Karla began when she called to schedule the next family meeting. "We'd like to talk to the kids about the plans. We think that they're old enough and mature enough for the conversation. You've always encouraged us to have this on our family agenda. Now's the time."

We arrived at the family's ranch house early one Friday morning. It had been the site of annual family meetings since the four kids were in their early teens. Today we would introduce the kids to Mike, who would serve as trustee when the time came. Karla and Joe greeted us and guided us into the kitchen, where the aroma of freshly brewed coffee warmed the atmosphere. Muffins and jam were set out for the taking. The household was slowly revving up to full speed.

One by one, Karla and Joe's four children wandered downstairs as an antique grandfather clock could be heard ticking in its corner of the dining room. While the family cat lay curled on a cozy pillow in the corner, we all sat together at the big round oak table. Tina, Chris, James, and Sonja were all in their twenties. Tina and Chris had finished college and were working. James had a part-time job and had taken time away from his studies. Sonja was a budding chef. It was an informal atmosphere, yet everyone knew this family meeting had a purpose.

Karla started things off.

"I'm glad we could all get together this morning. Kids, your dad and I asked Linda and Mike to join us to help explain some plans Dad and I have made for the future. Your father has worked so hard all these years, and now that he wants to retire, we need to be sure we have everything organized."

"Your mother and I are fortunate to be able to look forward now to some time together now that you're all grown," Joe went on. He'd spent years building a successful real estate company. "We'd like to enjoy the fruits of our labor, but we also have to set aside some rainy day resources for you. That's what Linda and Mike are here to tell you about."

"Tina, Chris, James, and Sonja, it's good to see you again," I began. "It's been a few years since we had the financial education workshop. Tina and Chris, I understand you have your own 401(k) plans now. James and Sonja, I hear your personal budgets are coming along nicely. That's great progress. Now that the four of you are well on your way to being launched, your parents are ready to talk with you about their own future plans. That's the agenda for today's family meeting."

Tina and Sonja looked at one another with anxious glances. James squirmed. Chris reached for another muffin.

"I know this group isn't shy. You've been meeting like this since you were young teens. So the same rules apply. Ask any questions that are on your mind. Nothing is off limits," I reminded them, realizing that it always takes a few minutes for everyone to get back in the family meeting mind-set.

"Your parents have worked extremely hard to achieve what they have from both a family and financial planning standpoint. With that good fortune comes the need to plan for what will happen after they pass on. That's what estate planning does.

"I think you all know by now that you kids have always been what's most important to your parents. They've decided that having an open discussion with you now about exactly how things will work in the future is the right step," I continued. "It fits with your family philosophy of 'share and share alike.'

"Many people do an estate plan—a will and a trust—but never tell their family members or anyone else what they did. Your parents have worked with their lawyer to prepare a very thoughtful plan and to set up trusts for each of you. Now they want you to learn about estate planning and about the trust they have established for your benefit.

"Your parents have also been very thoughtful, in my opinion, to arrange for Mike to oversee things as trustee. That means he will manage the property owned by the trust and will follow the instructions in the trust to make distributions to each of you, the beneficiaries, when the time comes. He'll be there to help.

"Mike, will you explain the estate plan in a bit more detail for everyone?" I said, turning the discussion over to Mike, an attorney by training who was an officer in a local trust company retained by Joe and Karla to administer their estate plan.

"Thanks, Linda," Mike began.

He continued, "A trust has been set up for each of you with funds to provide for your future. This transfers family assets from your parents to you. The trusts are identical, because your parents want you to be treated equally. The purpose of these trusts is not to provide you with income right away, but to give you a safety net for the future. Your parents are likely to live for a long time, and the assets they have put into these trusts are meant to stay there and grow for as long as your parents live."

Raising his hand slightly, Chris asked, "So does that mean we don't get to spend the money now?"

"Good question, Chris," Mike responded. He continued, "The way this works is that the trustee, the one overseeing the trusts, follows the instructions your parents set out in a legal document. There's no requirement to distribute anything to you yet. If you need funds for your health or further education, that would be considered. But the trustee will also consider your ability to be gainfully employed and provide those funds for yourself. As you know, your parents value hard work, and they want these resources to be available to you when you get to their stage in life."

Tina chimed in, "What's actually in a trust?"

"The trusts contain a combination of cash, stocks, and bonds. Your parents have not only worked hard and saved, but they also invested wisely through the years. Now they want to share part of their wealth with you," I explained.

"We've looked at investment portfolios together at past family meetings, for your college funds. These new accounts will be similar," I elaborated. "You'll be able to follow how the investments are doing, and your parents hope this will be interesting to you as well as educational."

Mike continued, "Your parents have also arranged for you to inherit the family's properties, eventually. But that won't happen now. You and your parents will continue to enjoy those places just as you do now."

Joe added, "I hope you'll keep the Tahoe house as a family gathering place. We've had some awesome times there. And it goes back to my grandfather's time."

I continued, "One of the things they'd like you all to think about are the family's other special possessions. That can be hard to do, but it's important to think about family heirlooms and what is most special to each of you. Your parents don't want any hard feelings later."

Karla continued," You know I have accumulated lots of jewelry over the years. You know, I'm a list maker. So I have a list of the pieces. I hope you'll think about it, and let me know if there are items that you like. I'm not handing over my diamonds now, mind you, but one day I might have grandchildren."

"I'm getting sad now," said Sonja. "I don't want to think about Mom and Dad not being around. Can we just not talk about this anymore?"

Karla interjected, her voice quivering, "I know it's a little scary, dear, but it's important you kids understand our wishes. And I really do want to know what household mementos you'd ultimately like to have. We can't read your mind, but your dad and I don't want to hurt anyone's feelings. What seems fair to us might not be what you'd choose."

"Yes, Sonja, your mom and dad are doing this so everything's clear for the future," I said, trying to reassure their youngest daughter, who still lived at home with Karla and Joe. "Mike has a packet of information for each of you that describes what we've talked about today. Legal terms can be a little off-putting, so he's included a glossary of definitions."

"Okay everyone, we've covered enough for now. Think about everything that's been discussed, and let us know if you have questions. And just like always, feel free to reach out to Linda if you'd rather run something by her first. She's your sounding board for our family meetings," said Joe, as he stood up from the table and hugged Karla. "Linda and Mike, thank you for being here today."

Karla smiled, handing each of her children a small box. "Take a muffin for the road! I've stashed the family recipe inside, too. It's from Grandma Kate."

Karla and Joe breathed a sigh of relief as the kids went on their way. It wouldn't be the last discussion about the family's succession plan, but a crucial step had been taken. When "who's getting what" is taken care of, the proverbial "elephant" is out of the room. When money questions are settled, the family can move on to other things, such as learning its history, sharing its memories, and telling its stories.

"Wait just a second, I have something I want to give you, Linda," Karla said as she opened the top drawer of the antique chest in the living room. "Joe and I have been working on this letter. Let us know if you think it's okay, and we'll give it to Mike to keep with our records."

Dear Tina, Chris, James, and Sonja,

First of all, remember our family promise, "No regrets." We know this time might be hard for you. After all, we've been together since day one. We made some wonderful memories. And we shared lots of laughs. We shared tears too, but we always stuck together. Now that's what the four of you must do.

We have no doubt that you'll do just fine in life. You're smart, honest, and kind. You follow the family credo well. You know how to treat others and how to make decisions when you reach a fork in the road. Your values are strong. You're grounded. Now your job is to be grateful.

And there's so much to be grateful for. Remember the fun times at Tahoe, like the day the big rope swing broke and James landed in the lake with a big splash. And the times the oven went on the blink, usually right before the turkey was ready to roast. Or when we thought Tina and Sonja were "lost" on the lake, but they were hiding in the boat with their summer boyfriends. Then Chris would always bring pounds of rocks home in his bag trying to keep summer alive. We hope your families will enjoy those beautiful sunsets for years to come.

There's a booklet of family recipes for each of you. Prepare with love. The photos are organized too, with copies for all. What we really want to give you is the sense of adventure that took us to so many places around the world. Hold on to your curiosity because it will keep you thinking and learning. Maintain an open mind, because others have a lot to teach you. Most important, keep your dreams alive. They give you hope.

Most important, keep laughing and loving, because that's what makes you happy.

Love,
Mom and Dad

*   *   *

Successful families aren't born that way. This is the good news and the bad news. There are no shortcuts. However, the route to success isn't a covert set of tactics reserved for the chosen few.

Having money isn't enough. Regardless of how wealth is defined, money alone can't buy happiness. Great families endure for generations through commitment to strong values and connections to each other.

"Hope" isn't a strategy for a business or for a family. Like a business, a family needs vision, energy, and laser-sharp focus on its goals in order to succeed. It takes good leadership and consistent work to ensure progress.

Today's business leaders understand that they key to a thriving enterprise is to get ideas and input from all the employees. Getting into the habit of always asking, "What should we do next?" is not only good for business; it's also good for your family.

Company directors appreciate that their most important responsibility is succession planning. Leaders of families must also educate and train the next generation because its turn is coming.

Trillions of dollars are changing hands as one generation makes way for another. I've been there after the wire transfers stop. What we want at that moment is not another bank statement, but the family stories.

If these riches get passed on, succession won't merely be about inheriting money. Truly staying rich can mean so much more.

This is the business of family.

Notes

1   Strategy: A Blueprint for Your Family

1. Bruce Upbin, "The Six Habits of Successful Private Companies," *Forbes*, June 30, 2013, http://www.forbes.com/sites/bruceupbin/2013/06/30/the-six-habits-of-successful-private-companies/ (accessed October 22, 2014).
2. Ibid.
3. Ibid.
4. Max Nisen, "Starbucks Has a Brilliant Strategy for Dominating the Chinese Market," *Business Insider*, October 31, 2012, http://www.businessinsider.com/starbucks-strategy-in-china-2012-10 (accessed October 22, 2014).
5. Jim Collins, *Good to Great: Why Some Companies Make the Leap…And Others Don't* (New York: HarperCollins, 2001), 16.

2   Mission: Keeping Your Family on Track

1. FranklinCovey, "Build a Mission Statement," http://www.franklincovey.com/msb/inspired/anonymous (accessed September 7, 2014).
2. Round Pond Estate, "Story," http://www.roundpond.com/the-family (accessed September 7, 2014).

3   Vision and Values: Put Family Members and Principles First

1. Jim Collins and Jerry I. Porras, *Built to Last: Successful Habits of Visionary Companies* (New York: HarperBusiness, 1994), 1.

4   Forging Family Partnerships

1. "Leading Through Connections: Insights from the IBM Global CEO Study," IBM.com, 2012, http://www-935.ibm.com/services/us/en/c-suite/ceostudy2012 (accessed October 28, 2014).
2. Karlee Weinmann and Aimee Groth, "The Ten Largest Family Businesses in America, *Business Insider,* November 17, 2011, http://www.businessinsider.com/the-10-largest-family-businesses-in-America-2011-11?op=1 (accessed October 28, 2014).
3. Albert Mehrabian, *Silent Messages: Implicit Communication of Emotions and Attitudes* (Belmont, CA: Wadsworth, 1981), 44.

4. Craig E. Aronoff, and John L. Ward, *Family Meetings: How to Build a Stronger Family and a Stronger Business* (New York: Palgrave Macmillan, 2011). 17.
5. Alex Pentland, "The Hard Science of Teamwork," *Harvard Business Review*, March 20, 2012, http://blogs.hbr.org/2012/03/the-new-science-building-gr (accessed October 26, 2014).
6. "Picture Your Legacy," produced by 21/64, Andrea and Charles Bronfman Philanthropies, http://21/64.net/store/tool/picture-your-legacy (accessed October 29, 2014).

5 Setting Goals and Celebrating Milestones

1. Earl Nightingale, *The Strangest Secret* (Melrose, FL: Laurenzana Press, [1994] 2011), 18.

6 Every Family Member Matters: Roles, Responsibilities, and Making Decisions

1. Daniela Montemerlo and John L. Ward, *The Family Constitution: Agreements to Secure and Perpetuate Your Family and Your Business* (New York: Palgrave Macmillan, 2011), xiii.
2. "The Family Constitution Guide," Taylor Wessing, http://www.taylorwessing.com/fileadmin/files/docs/Family_Constitution_Guide.pdf, 5 (accessed October 28, 2014).
3. Ibid., 6.
4. Montemerlo and Ward, *The Family Constitution*, 5.

7 Family IQ: Education and Training

1. Josh Bersin, "Spending on Corporate Training Soars: Employee Capabilities Now a Priority," *Forbes*, February 2, 2014, http://www.forbes.com/sites/joshbersin/2014/02/04/the-recovery-arrives-corporate-training-spend-skyrockets/ (accessed November 5, 2014).
2. Laura Raines, "Companies that Invest in Employee Education Reap Multiple Benefits," *Atlanta Journal-Constitution*, March 29, 2012, http://www.ajc.com/news/business/companies-that-invest-in-employee-education-reap-m/nQSd4/ (accessed November 5, 2014); UPS website, "Working at UPS: Benefits," https://ups.managehr.com/benefits.htm (accessed November 5, 2014).
3. Josh Bersin, "Millennials Will Soon Rule the World: But How Will They Lead?" *Forbes*, September 12, 2013, http://www.forbes.com/sites/joshbersin/2013/09/12/millenials-will-soon-rule-the-world-but-how-will-they-lead/ (accessed November 5, 2014).
4. John J. Havens and Paul G. Schervish, "A Golden Age of Philanthropy Still Beckons: National Wealth Transfer and Potential for Philanthropy Technical Report," Center on Wealth and Philanthropy, Boston College, May 28, 2014, http://www.bc.edu/content/dam/files/research_sites/cwp/pdf/A%20Golden%20Age%20of%20Philanthropy%20Still%20Bekons.pdf, 27 (accessed November 5, 2014).
5. Blaire Briody, "SAT Tests: Another Drain on the Family Budget," *The Fiscal Times*, May 1, 2013, http://www.thefiscaltimes.com/Articles/2013/05/01/SAT-Tests-Another-Drain-on-the-Family-Budge (accessed November 5, 2014).

6. Nimi Akinkugbe, "Raising Financially Literate Children," *Businessday Online,* August 25, 2014, http://businessdayonline.com/2014/08/raising-financially-literate -children/#.VFvKjij89KM (accessed November 5, 2014).

7. Joline Godfrey, *Raising Financially Fit Kids* (Berkeley, CA: Ten Speed Press, 2010), 27.

8. Elaine King, WE Family Offices, http://www.wefamilyoffices.com/team/elaine -king/ (accessed November 5, 2014).

9. Susan Gunelius, "Women Making Economic Strides and Not Slowing Down," *Forbes,* July 28, 2010, http://www.forbes.com/sites/work-in-progress/2010/07/28 /women-making-economic-strides-and-not-slowing-down/ (accessed November 5, 2014); Martha Barletta, "Capture the Power of the Purse," *Quirk's Marketing Research Review,* 19, no. 2 (February 2005): 52; Lauren Ohayon, "Women and Investing," *That Money Show,* October 2000, http://www.pbs.org/wnet/moneyshow/cover/102000. html (accessed November 5, 2014).

10. Dan Hurley, "Divorce Rate: It's Not as High as You Think," *New York Times,* April 19, 2005, http://www.nytimes.com/2005/04/19/health/19divo.html_r=0 (accessed October 29, 2014); Mark Banschick, "The High Failure Rate of Second and Third Marriages," *Psychology Today,* February 6, 2012, http://www.psychologytoday .com/blog/the-intelligent-divorce/201202/the-high failure-rate-second-and-third -marriages (accessed November 10, 2014); Sharon Kedar and Manisha Thakor, *Get Financially Naked: How to Talk Money with Your Honey,* (Avon, MA: Adams Media, 2009), xix; Hadley Malcolm, "Women's Financial Power Grows Faster Than Savvy," *USA Today,* August 17, 2012, http://usatoday30.usatoday.com/money/perfi/basics /story/2012-08-16/womens-financial-literacy-confidence/57104200/1 (accessed November 9, 2014).

8 Family EQ: Getting Along to Get Ahead

1. "The Transfer of Trust: Wealth & Succession in a Changing World," Barclays Wealth Insights, 2011, https://wealth.barclays.com/content/dam/bwpublic/americas /documents/wealth_management/insights14-the-transfer-of-trust-BWA.pdf (accessed November 9, 2014).

2. Roy Williams and Vic Preisser, *Preparing Heirs: Five Steps to a Successful Transition of Family Wealth and Values* (San Francisco: Robert Reed, 2003), 49.

3. "The Transfer of Trust," Barclays Wealth Insights.

4. KPMG Enterprise, Centre for Family Business, http://www.kpmg.com/ca/en /services/kpmg-enterprise/centre-for-family-business/pages/default.aspx (accessed November 9, 2014).

5. "Psych Basics: What is Emotional Intelligence?" *Psychology Today,* http://www.psy- chologytoday.com/basics/emotional-intelligence (accessed November 9, 2014).

6. Lee Hausner and Douglas K. K. Freeman, *The Legacy Family: The Definitive Guide to Creating a Successful Multigenerational Family* (New York: Palgrave Macmillan, 2009).

7. Heather Zynczak, "Going Global: 4 Major Management Challenges and How to Cope," LinkedIn, March 25, 2014, http://www.linkedin.com/today/post /article/20140325200143-1687653-going-global-4-major-management-challenges -and-how-to-cope?trk=mp-reader-card (accessed November 9, 2014).

8. Boris Groysberg and Michael Slind, "The Silent Killer of Big Companies," *Harvard Business Review* blog, October 25, 2012, https://hbr.org/2012/10/the-silent-killer -of-big-companies/ (accessed November 9, 2014).

9 Family Audit: Guidance and Mentoring

1. International Coach Federation, "ICF Global Coaching Client Survey: Executive Summary," 2009, http://icf.files.cms-plus.com/includes/media/docs/ExecutiveSummary.pdf (accessed November 9, 2014).
2. James E. Hughes, "A Reflection on the Art and Practice of Mentorship," 2002, http://www.jamesehughes.com/articles/Mentorship.pdf (accessed November 9, 2014); James E. Hughes, *Family Wealth: Keeping It in the Family* (New York: John Wiley, 2002), 164, 89.
3. Christophe Bernard, "Mentoring the Next Generation for the Future Success of the Business," KPMG Family Business, February 3, 2014, http://www.kpmgfamilybusiness.com/mentoring-next-generation-future-success-business/ (accessed November 9, 2014).
4. Mark Haynes Daniell, *Strategy for the Wealthy Family: Seven Principles to Assure Riches to Riches Across Generations* (New York: John Wiley, 2008), 83.
5. Rachel Gall, "About Millennials," *So-Called Millennial* website, http://socalledmillennial.com/about/ (accessed November 9, 2014).
6. Rose Kumar, "Up Close and Personal with the Millennial Stress Generation," *Huffington Post,* September 28, 2014, http://www.huffingtonpost.com/rose-kumar-md/millennials-stress_b_2766829.html (accessed November 9, 2014).
7. Suniya S. Luthar, "The Problem with Rich Kids," *Psychology Today* (November-December 2013): 62–69.
8. James E. Hughes, *Family Wealth: Keeping It in the Family,* 165.

10 Financial Sustainability: Working with Your Money, Not against It

1. Paula Pant, "Top 10 Biggest Investment Failures Ever," *Daily Finance,* May 8, 2014, http://www.dailyfinance.com/2014/05/08/biggest-investment-failures-ever/ (accessed November 20, 2014).
2. "The Worst Business Decisions of All Time," 24/7wallst.com, October 17, 2012, http://247wallst.com/special-report/2012/10/17/the-worst-business-decisions-of-all-time/ (accessed November 20, 2014).
3. "Those Medici," *The Economist,* December 23, 1999, http://www.economist.com/node/347333 (accessed November 20, 2014).
4. "The World's Most Admired Companies," *Fortune,* March 17, 2014, http://fortune.com/worlds-most-admired-companies/apple-1/ (accessed November 20, 2014).
5. François M. de Visscher, "Seven Habits of Highly Effective Companies," UMass Amherst Family Business Center, 2014, http://www.umass.edu/fambiz/articles/money_issues/seven_habits.html (accessed November 20, 2014).
6. Robb Silverblatt, "Are There Too Many Mutual Funds?" *US News,* "Money," June 10, 2013, http://money.usnews.com/money/personal-finance/mutual-funds/articles/2013/06/10/are-there-too-many-mutual-funds (accessed November 20, 2014).
7. "2013 Quantitative Analysis of Investor Behavior," DALBAR, http://www.quaib.com/public/default.aspx (accessed November 20, 2014).
8. Paul Sullivan, "The Folklore of Finance: Beliefs That Contribute to Investors' Failure," *New York Times,* November 15, 2014, http://www.nytimes.com/2014/11/15/your-money/decision-making-methods-obstruct-path-to-investment-goals.html?_r=0 (accessed November 20, 2014).

9. Kevin Cavanaugh and Roger Gewecke, "Why Investors Don't Earn the Returns They Should," Clifford Swan Investment Counsel, October 16, 2014.

10. "All in the Family," World Finance.com, September 5, 2012, http://www.worldfinance .com/home/special-reports-home/all-in-the-family-2 (accessed November 20, 2014).

11. Charles Schwab, *The Age of Independent Advice: The Remarkable History of the Independent Advisor Industry* (San Francisco: Charles Schwab Corp., 2007), 20–21.

12. Russ Alan Prince, "Robo-Advisor 3.0: A Family Office for Everyone," *Forbes,* November 12, 2014, http://www.forbes.com/sites/russalanprince/2014/11/12/robo -advisor-3-0-a-family-office-for-everyone/ (accessed November 20, 2014).

11 Family Sustainability: Risk and Resilience

1. Steven Slezak, "GM's Risk Management Failures Provide Lessons for Other Firms," Globalriskinsights.com, March 14, 2014, http://globalriskinsights.com/2014/03/gms -risk-management-failures-provide-example-for-other-firms/ (accessed November 23, 2014).

2. Robert S. Kaplan and Anette Mikes, "Managing Risks: A New Framework," *Harvard Business Review,* June 2012, https://hbr.org/2012/06/managing-risks-a-new -framework (accessed November 23, 2014).

3. Enterprise Risk Management Initiative Staff, "How Did BP's Risk Management Lead to Failure?" North Carolina State University, Poole College of Management, July 1, 2010, http://erm.ncsu.edu/library/article/bp-risk-management#.VHIjcij89KM (accessed November 23, 2014).

4. Mallen Baker, "Companies in Crisis – What Not to Do When it All Goes Wrong," Corporate Social Responsibility, http://www.mallenbaker.net/csr/crisis03.html.

5. "Not Guilty After All," *The Economist,* June 2, 2005, http://www.economist.com /node/4033756 (accessed November 23, 2014).

6. Kaplan and Mikes, "Managing Risks: A New Framework," *Harvard Business Review,* June, 2012.

7. *Financial Advisor* Staff, "HNW Clients Have Heightened Health Care Concerns, Survey Says," *Financial Advisor Magazine,* November 14, 2014, http://www.fa-mag .com/news/wealthy-concerned-about-health-19891.html (accessed November 23, 2014).

8. "Do Wealthy Families Really Need More Insurance?" oyerinsurance.com, May 13, 2014, http://www.oyerinsurance.com/wealthy-families-need-insurance/ (accessed November 23, 2014).

9. Gary Raphael, "5 Big Security Risks for HNW Families," *Think Advisor,* September 18, 2012, http://www.thinkadvisor.com/2012/09/18/5-big-security-risks-for-hnw-families (accessed November 23, 2014).

10. "Everything You Need to Know about Prenuptial Agreements," Bankrate.com, May 10, 2006, http://www.bankrate.com/brm/prenup.asp (accessed November 23, 2014).

11. Henry Gornbein, "Prenuptial Agreements: The Good, The Bad, and the Ugly," *Huffington Post,* November 21, 2014, http://www.huffingtonpost.com/henry-gornbein /prenuptial-agreements-the_b_1088748.html (accessed November 23, 2014).

12. "The Road to Resilience, What is Resilience," American Psychological Association, 2014, http://www.apa.org/helpcenter/road-resilience.aspx (accessed November 23, 2014).

13. Paul Tough, *How Children Succeed* (New York: Houghton Mifflin Harcourt, 2012), 13–14.

14. Libby Sander, "As Crises Mount, a Push for Communities to Focus on Resilience," *The Chronicle of Philanthropy* 27, no. 3 (November 2014): 1, 12.
15. Judith Rodin, *The Resilience Dividend: Being Strong in a World Where Things Go Wrong* (New York: Public Affairs, 2014), 9–39.

12   Family Dividends: Gratitude and Legacy

1. Committee Encouraging Corporate Philanthropy, *Giving In Numbers: 2013 Edition*, http://www.pointsoflight.org/sites/default/files/resources/files/2012_giving_in_numbers_cecp.pdf, 8 (accessed November 14, 2014).
2. Committee Encouraging Corporate Philanthropy, *CECP Remembers Paul Newman*, CECP website video, http://cecp.co/about-cecp/board-of-directors/paul-newman.html (accessed November 14, 2014).
3. Lilly Family School of Philanthropy, "Giving Beyond Borders: A Study of Global Giving by U.S. Corporations," October 2013, http://www.philanthropy.iupui.edu/files/file/giving_beyond_borders_-_global_impact_iu_study_final.pdf, 9 (accessed November 14, 2014).
4. "Entrepreneurs are More Likely to Give to Charity," Fidelity Charitable, November 12, 2010, http://www.fidelitycharitable.org/about-us/news/11-12-2010.shtml (accessed November 25, 2014).
5. Daniel Stimson, "Inner Workings of the Magnanimous Mind," National Institutes of Health, April 4, 2007, http://www.ninds.nih.gov/news_and_events/news_articles/brain_activity_during_altruism.htm (accessed November 14, 2014).
6. Paul J. Zak, "The Moral Molecule: Neuroscience and Economic Behavior," *Psychology Today,* September 8, 2011, http://www.psychologytoday.com/blog/the-moral-molecule, (accessed November 14, 2014).
7. Kara Ohngren Prior, "9 Famous Entrepreneur Philanthropists," Entrepreneur.com, 2012, http://www.entrepreneur.com/slideshow/224215 (accessed November 14, 2014).
8. Eliane Chavagnon, "Study of High Net Worth Philanthropy," *Family Wealth Report,* October 21, 2014, http://www.fwreport.com/article_print_preview.php?id=50409 (accessed November 14, 2014).
9. Robert T. Napier, "Private Foundations and Donor Advised Funds," Wealth Management.com, May 21, 2014, http://wealthmanagement.com/estate-planning/private-foundations-and-donor-advised-funds (accessed November 14, 2014).
10. "American History's Greatest Philanthropists," Philanthropy Roundtable.org, Winter 2014, http://www.philanthropyroundtable.org/topic/excellence_in_philanthropy/american_historys_great_philanthropists (accessed November 24, 2014).
11. Center on Philanthropy at Indiana University, "Giving USA 2012: The Annual Report on Philanthropy for the Year 2011," Giving USA Foundation, http://www.etsu.edu/125/documents/GIVING%20USA%202012.pdf (accessed November 14, 2014).
12. Veronica Dagher, "Talking Philanthropy with Millennials," *Wall Street Journal,* September 19, 2014, http://online.wsj.com/articles/talking-philanthropy-with-millennials-1411132805?tesla=y&mg=reno64- (accessed November 14, 2014).
13. Trevor Neilson, "Philanthropy and Millennials: Get on Board or Get Left Behind," *Huffington Post,* June 6, 2013, http://www.huffingtonpost.com/trevor-neilson/philanthrop-and-millennia_b_3269238.html (accessed November 14, 2014).

13 Family R&D: Preparing the Next Generation

1. Battelle, "2014 Global R&D Funding Forecast," December 2013, http://www.battelle
.org/docs/tpp/2014_global_rd_funding_forecast.pdf (accessed November 15, 2014).
2. Judy Martel, "Five Wealthy Families Who Lost Their Fortunes," Bankrate.com,
http://www.bankrate.com/finance/smart-spending/wealthy-families-who-lost
-their-fortunr-1.aspx#ixzz3J5oXbhIn (accessed November 15, 2014).
3. Robert Safian, "The World's Most Innovative Companies 2014," *Fast Company*,
October 7, 2014, http://www.fastcompany.com/3026098/most-innovative-companies
-2014/the-worlds-most-innovative-companies-2014 (accessed November 15, 2014).
4. Tabasco, http://www.tabasco.com/mcilhenny-company/about/ (accessed November 15,
2014).
5. Ibid.
6. Alice Boyes, "25 Travel Quotes," *Psychology Today*, January 2, 2013, http://www
.psychologytoday.com/blog/in-practice/201301/25-travel-quotes.
7. Pierre Gurdjian, Thomas Halbeisen, and Kevin Lane, "Why Leadership-
Development Programs Fail," *McKinsey Quarterly*, January 2014, http://www
.mckinsey.com/insights/leading_in_the_21st_century/why_leadership-development
_programs_fail (accessed November 15, 2014).
8. Stephen P. Miller, "Developing Next Generation Leaders in Family Businesses,"
The Family Business Consulting Group, November 2, 2014, http://www.thefbcg
.com/developing-next-generation-leaders-in-family-business/ (accessed November 15,
2014).
9. Adriana Gardella, "Family Businesses Learn to Adapt to Keep Thriving," *New
York Times*, April 4, 2012, http://www.nytimes.com/2012/04/05/business
/smallbusiness/how-they-beat-the-odds-to-keep-family-businesses-healthy
.html?pagewanted=all&_r=0 (accessed November 25, 2014).

14 The Future of Your Family: No Success without Succession

1. Darcy Jacobsen, "Your Succession Plan Stinks: Tips for Finding and Developing
HiPos in Your Company," *Globoforce*, August 11, 2014, http://www.globoforce
.com/gfblog/2014/your-succession-plan-stinks/ (accessed November 16, 2014).
2. David Roady and Gordon McCoun, "CEO Transitions," *FTI Journal*, December
2011, http://ftijournal.com/article/ceo-transitions (accessed November 16, 2014).
3. Jacobsen, "Your Succession Plan Stinks."
4. Kendra Thompson, "Wealth Transfer: Why It's a More Timely Topic Now Than
Ever Before," *Accenture*, April 23, 2014, www.accenture.com/us-en/blogs/accenture
-wealth-and-asset-management-blog/archive/2014/04/17/wealth-transfer-why-its
-a-more-timely-topic-now-than-eever-before.aspx (accessed November 16, 2014).
5. Douglas McIntyre, "The Ten Most Infamous Family Inheritance Feuds," *Daily
Finance*, June 6, 2011, http://www.dailyfinance.com/2011/06/06/the-10-most
-infamous-family-inheritance-feuds/ (accessed November 16, 2014).
6. Leah Goldman, "10 Celebrities Who Made Terrible Mistakes When Planning
Their Estates," *Business Insider*, December 7, 2010, http://www.businessinsider.
com/celebrity-estate-mistakes-2010-12?op=1 (accessed November 17, 2014).

Bibliography

"2013 Quantitative Analysis of Investor Behavior." DALBAR. http://www.quaib.com /public/default.aspx (accessed November 20, 2014).

Akinkugbe, Nimi. "Raising Financially Literate Children." *Businessday Online,* August 25, 2014. http://businessdayonline.com/2014/08/raising-financially-literate-children /#.VFvKjij89KM (accessed November 5, 2014).

"All in the Family." World Finance.com, September 5, 2012. http://www.worldfinance .com/home/special-reports-home/all-in-the-family-2 (accessed November 20, 2014).

"American History's Greatest Philanthropists." Philanthropy Roundtable.org, Winter 2014. http://www.philanthropyroundtable.org/topic/excellence_in_philanthropy /american_historys_great_philanthropists (accessed November 24, 2014).

Aronoff, Craig E., and John L. Ward. *Family Meetings: How to Build a Stronger Family and a Stronger Business.* New York: Palgrave Macmillan, 2011.

Baker, Mallen. "Companies in Crisis – What Not to Do When It All Goes Wrong." Corporate Social Responsibility. http://www.mallenbaker.net/csr/crisis03.html (accessed November 24, 2014).

Banschick, Mark. "The High Failure Rate of Second and Third Marriages." *Psychology Today,* February 6, 2012. http://www.psychologytoday.com/blog/the-intelligent -divorce/201202/the-high failure-rate-second-and-third-marriages (accessed November 10, 2014).

Barletta, Martha. "Capture the Power of the Purse." *Quirk's Marketing Research Review* 19, no. 2 (February 2005): 52–55.

Battelle. "2014 Global R&D Funding Forecast." December 2013. http://www.battelle. org/docs/tpp/2014_global_rd_funding_forecast.pdf (accessed November 15, 2014).

Bernard, Christophe. "Mentoring the Next Generation for the Future Success of the Business." *KPMG Family Business,* February 3, 2014. http://www.kpmgfamilybusiness .com/mentoring-next-generation-future-success-business/ (accessed November 9, 2014).

Bersin, Josh. "Millennials Will Soon Rule the World: But How Will They Lead?" *Forbes,* September 12, 2013. http://www.forbes.com/sites/joshbersin/2013/09/12/millenials -will-soon-rule-the-world-but-how-will-they-lead/ (accessed November 5, 2014).

Bersin, Josh. "Spending on Corporate Training Soars: Employee Capabilities Now a Priority." *Forbes,* February 2, 2014. http://www.forbes.com/sites/joshbersin /2014/02/04/the-recovery-arrives-corporate-training-spend-skyrockets/ (accessed November 5, 2014).

Boyes, Alice. "25 Travel Quotes." *Psychology Today,* January 2, 2013. http://www
.psychologytoday.com/blog/in-practice/201301/25-travel-quotes (accessed November 15,
2014).

Cavanaugh, Kevin, and Roger Gewecke. "Why Investors Don't Earn the Returns They
Should." *Clifford Swan Investment Counsel,* October 16, 2014.

Briody, Blaire. "SAT Tests: Another Drain on the Family Budget." *The Fiscal Times,* May 1,
2013. http://www.thefiscaltimes.com/Articles/2013/05/01/SAT-Tests-Another-Drain
-on-the-Family-Budge (accessed November 5, 2014).

Center on Philanthropy at Indiana University. "Giving USA 2012: The Annual Report
on Philanthropy for the Year 2011." Giving USA Foundation. http://www.etsu
.edu/125/documents/GIVING%20USA%202012.pdf (accessed November 14, 2014).

Chavagnon, Eliane. "Study of High Net Worth Philanthropy." *Family Wealth Report,*
October 21, 2014. http://www.fwreport.com/article_print_preview.php?id=50409
(accessed November 14, 2014).

Collins, Jim. *Good to Great: Why Some Companies Make the Leap...And Others Don't.*
New York: HarperCollins, 2001.

Collins, Jim, and Jerry I. Porras. *Built to Last: Successful Habits of Visionary Companies.*
New York: HarperBusiness, 1994.

Committee Encouraging Corporate Philanthropy. *CECP Remembers Paul Newman.*
CECP website video. http://cecp.co/about-cecp/board-of-directors/paul-newman
.html (accessed November 14, 2014).

Committee Encouraging Corporate Philanthropy. *Giving In Numbers: 2013 Edition.*
http://www.pointsoflight.org/sites/default/files/resources/files/2012_giving_in
_numbers_cecp.pdf (accessed November 14, 2014).

Dagher, Veronica. "Talking Philanthropy with Millennials." *Wall Street Journal,*
September 19, 2014. http://online.wsj.com/articles/talking-philanthropy-with
-millennials-1411132805?tesla=y&mg=reno64- (accessed November 14, 2014).

Daniell, Mark Haynes. *Strategy for the Wealthy Family: Seven Principles to Assure Riches
to Riches Across Generations.* New York: John Wiley, 2008.

"Do Wealthy Families Really Need More Insurance?" oyerinsurance.com, May 13,
2014. http://www.oyerinsurance.com/wealthy-families-need-insurance/ (accessed
November 23, 2014).

Enterprise Risk Management Initiative Staff. "How Did BP's Risk Management Lead to
Failure?" North Carolina State University, Poole College of Management, July 1, 2010.
http://erm.ncsu.edu/library/article/bp-risk-management#.VHIjcij89KM (accessed
November 23, 2014).

"Entrepreneurs are More Likely to Give to Charity," Fidelity Charitable, November 12,
2010, http://www.fidelitycharitable.org/about-us/news/11-12-2010.shtml (accessed
November 25, 2014).

"Everything You Need to Know about Prenuptial Agreements." Bankrate.com, May 10,
2006. http://www.bankrate.com/brm/prenup.asp (accessed November 23, 2014).

"The Family Constitution Guide." Taylor Wessing. http://www.taylorwessing.com
/fileadmin/files/docs/Family_Constitution_Guide.pdf (accessed October 28, 2014).

Financial Advisor Staff. "HNW Clients Have Heightened Health Care Concerns, Survey
Says." *Financial Advisor Magazine,* November 14, 2014. http://www.fa-mag.com
/news/wealthy-concerned-about-health-19891.html (accessed November 23, 2014).

FranklinCovey. "Build a Mission Statement." http://www.franklincovey.com/msb
/inspired/anonymous (accessed September 7, 2014).

Gall, Rachel. "About Millennials." *So-Called Millennial* website. http://socalledmillennial.com/about/ (accessed November 9, 2014).

Gardella, Adriana. "Family Businesses Learn to Adapt to Keep Thriving." *New York Times,* April 4, 2012. http://www.nytimes.com/2012/04/05/business/smallbusiness/how-they-beat-the-odds-to-keep-family-businesses-healthy.html?pagewanted=all&_r=0 (accessed November 25, 2014).

Godfrey, Joline. *Raising Financially Fit Kids.* Berkeley, CA: Ten Speed Press, 2010.

Goldman, Leah. "10 Celebrities Who Made Terrible Mistakes When Planning Their Estates." *Business Insider,* December 7, 2010. http://www.businessinsider.com/celebrity-estate-mistakes-2010-12?op=1 (accessed November 17, 2014).

Gornbein, Henry. "Prenuptial Agreements: The Good, The Bad, and the Ugly," *Huffington Post,* November 21, 2014. http://www.huffingtonpost.com/henry-gornbein/prenuptial-agreements-the_b_1088748.html (accessed November 23, 2014).

Groysberg, Boris, and Michael Slind. "The Silent Killer of Big Companies." *Harvard Business Review* blog, October 25, 2012. https://hbr.org/2012/10/the-silent-killer-of-big-companies/ (accessed November 9, 2014).

Gunelius, Susan. "Women Making Economic Strides and Not Slowing Down." *Forbes,* July 28, 2010. http://www.forbes.com/sites/work-in-progress/2010/07/28/women-making-economic-strides-and-not-slowing-down/ (accessed November 5, 2014).

Gurdjian, Pierre, Thomas Halbeisen, and Kevin Lane. "Why Leadership-Development Programs Fail." *McKinsey Quarterly,* January 2014. http://www.mckinsey.com/insights/leading_in_the_21st_century/why_leadership-development_programs_fail (accessed November 15, 2014).

Hausner, Lee, and Douglas K. K. Freeman. *The Legacy Family: The Definitive Guide to Creating a Successful Multigenerational Family.* New York: Palgrave Macmillan, 2009.

Havens, John J., and Paul G. Schervish. "A Golden Age of Philanthropy Still Beckons: National Wealth Transfer and Potential for Philanthropy Technical Report." Center on Wealth and Philanthropy, Boston College, May 28, 2014. http://www.bc.edu/content/dam/files/research_sites/cwp/pdf/A%20Golden%20Age%20of%20Philanthropy%20Still%20Bekons.pdf (accessed November 5, 2014).

Hughes, James E. "A Reflection on the Art and Practice of Mentorship." 2002. http://www.jamesehughes.com/articles/Mentorship.pdf (accessed November 9, 2014).

Hughes, James E. *Family Wealth: Keeping It in the Family.* New York: John Wiley, 2002.

Hurley, Dan. "Divorce Rate: It's Not as High as You Think." *New York Times,* April 19, 2005. http://www.nytimes.com/2005/04/19/health/19divo.html_r=0 (accessed October 29, 2014).

International Coach Federation. "ICF Global Coaching Client Survey: Executive Summary." 2009. http://icf.files.cms-plus.com/includes/media/docs/ExecutiveSummary.pdf (accessed November 9, 2014).

Jacobsen, Darcy. "Your Succession Plan Stinks: Tips for Finding and Developing HiPos in Your Company." *Globoforce,* August 11, 2014. http://www.globoforce.com/gfblog/2014/your-succession-plan-stinks/ (accessed November 16, 2014).

Jennings, Will. "The Olympics as a Story of Risk Management." *Harvard Business Review,* August 13, 2012. http://hbr.org/2012/08/the-olympics-as-a-story-of-ris (accessed November 23, 2014).

Kaplan, Robert S., and Anette Mikes. "Managing Risks: A New Framework." *Harvard Business Review,* June 2012. https://hbr.org/2012/06/managing-risks-a-new-framework (accessed November 23, 2014).

Kedar, Sharon, and Manisha Thakor. *Get Financially Naked: How to Talk Money with Your Honey.* Avon, MA: Adams Media, 2009.

King, Elaine. WE Family Offices. http://www.wefamilyoffices.com/team/elaine-king/ (accessed November 5, 2014).

Kotz, Deborah. "11 Health Habits that Will Help You Live to 100." *US News & World Report,* February 20, 2009. http://health.usnews.com/health-news/family-health /living-well/articles/2009/02/20/10-health-habits-that-will-help-you-live-to-100 (accessed November 23, 2014).

KPMG Enterprise. Centre for Family Business. http://www.kpmg.com/ca/en/services /kpmg-enterprise/centre-for-family-business/pages/default.aspx (accessed November 9, 2014).

Kumar, Rose. "Up Close and Personal with the Millennial Stress Generation." *Huffington Post,* September 28, 2014. http://www.huffingtonpost.com/rose-kumar-md/millennials -stress_b_2766829.html (accessed November 9, 2014).

"Leading Through Connections: Insights from the IBM Global CEO Study." IBM. com, 2012. http://www-935.ibm.com/services/us/en/c-suite/ceostudy2012 (accessed October 28, 2014).

Lilly Family School of Philanthropy. "Giving Beyond Borders: A Study of Global Giving by U.S. Corporations." October 2013. http://www.philanthropy.iupui.edu/files/file/giving _beyond_borders_-_global_impact_iu_study_final.pdf (accessed November 14, 2014).

Luthar, Suniya S. "The Problem with Rich Kids." *Psychology Today* (November-December 2013): 62–69.

Malcolm, Hadley. "Women's Financial Power Grows Faster than Savvy." *USA Today,* August 17, 2012. http://usatoday30.usatoday.com/money/perfi/basics/story/2012-08-16/ womens-financial-literacy-confidence/57104200/1 (accessed November 9, 2014).

Martel, Judy. "Five Wealthy Families Who Lost Their Fortunes." Bankrate.com. http:// www.bankrate.com/finance/smart-spending/wealthy-families-who-lost-their-fortunr -1.aspx#ixzz3J5oXbhIn (accessed November 15, 2014).

McIntyre, Douglas. "The Ten Most Infamous Family Inheritance Feuds." *Daily Finance,* June 6, 2011. http://www.dailyfinance.com/2011/06/06/the-10-most-infamous-family -inheritance-feuds/ (accessed November 16, 2014).

Mehrabian, Albert. *Silent Messages: Implicit Communication of Emotions and Attitudes.* Belmont, CA: Wadsworth Publishing Company, 1981.

Miller, Stephen P. "Developing Next Generation Leaders in Family Businesses." The Family Business Consulting Group, November 2, 2014. http://www.thefbcg.com /developing-next-generation-leaders-in-family-business/ (accessed November 15, 2014).

Montemerlo, Daniela, and John L. Ward. *The Family Constitution: Agreements to Secure and Perpetuate Your Family and Your Business.* New York: Palgrave Macmillan, 2011.

Napier, Robert T. "Private Foundations and Donor Advised Funds." Wealth Management.com, May 21, 2014. http://wealthmanagement.com/estate-planning /private-foundations-and-donor-advised-funds (accessed November 14, 2014).

Neilson, Trevor. "Philanthropy and Millennials: Get on Board or Get Left Behind." *Huffington Post,* June 6, 2013. http://www.huffingtonpost.com/trevor-neilson /philanthrop-and-millennia_b_3269238.html (accessed November 14, 2014).

Nightingale, Earl. The Strangest Secret. Melrose, FL:Laurenzana Press, (1994) 2011.

Nike. http://www.nikeresponsibility.com/timeline/ (accessed November 15, 2014).

Nisen, Max. "Starbucks Has a Brilliant Strategy for Dominating the Chinese Market." *Business Insider,* October 31, 2012. http://www.businessinsider.com/starbucks-strategy -in-china-2012-10 (accessed October 22, 2014).

"Not Guilty After All." *The Economist,* June 2, 2005. http://www.economist.com/node/4033756 (accessed November 23, 2014).

Ohayon, Lauren. "Women and Investing." *That Money Show,* October 2000. http://www.pbs.org/wnet/moneyshow/cover/102000.html (accessed November 5, 2014).

Pant, Paula. "Top 10 Biggest Investment Failures Ever." *Daily Finance,* May 8, 2014. http://www.dailyfinance.com/2014/05/08/biggest-investment-failures-ever/ (accessed November 20, 2014).

Pentland, Alex. "The Hard Science of Teamwork." *Harvard Business Review,* March 20, 2012. http://blogs.hbr.org/2012/03/the-new-science-building-gr (accessed October 26, 2014).

"Picture Your Legacy." 21/64, Andrea and Charles Bronfman Philanthropies. http://21.64.net/store/tool/picture-your-legacy (accessed October 29, 2014).

Prince, Russ Alan. "Robo-Advisor 3.0: A Family Office for Everyone." *Forbes,* November 12, 2014. http://www.forbes.com/sites/russalanprince/2014/11/12/robo-advisor-3-0-a-family-office-for-everyone/ (accessed November 20, 2014).

Prior, Kara Ohngren. "9 Famous Entrepreneur Philanthropists." Entrepreneur.com, 2012. http://www.entrepreneur.com/slideshow/224215 (accessed November 14, 2014).

"Psych Basics: What is Emotional Intelligence?" *Psychology Today.* http://www.psychologytoday.com/basics/emotional-intelligence (accessed November 9, 2014).

Raines, Laura. "Companies that Invest in Employee Education Reap Multiple Benefits." *Atlanta Journal-Constitution,* March 29, 2012. http://www.ajc.com/news/business/companies-that-invest-in-employee-education-reap-m/nQSd4/ (accessed November 5, 2014).

Raphael, Gary. "5 Big Security Risks for HNW Families." *Think Advisor,* September 18, 2012. http://www.thinkadvisor.com/2012/09/18/5-big-security-risks-for-hnw-families (accessed November 23, 2014).

"The Road to Resilience, What is Resilience." American Psychological Association, 2014. http://www.apa.org/helpcenter/road-resilience.aspx (accessed November 23, 2014).

Roady, David, and Gordon McCoun. "CEO Transitions." *FTI Journal,* December 2011. http://ftijournal.com/article/ceo-transitions (accessed November 16, 2014).

Rodin, Judith. *The Resilience Dividend: Being Strong in a World Where Things Go Wrong.* New York: Public Affairs, 2014.

Round Pond Estate. "Story." http://www.roundpond.com/the-family (accessed September 7, 2014).

Safian, Robert. "The World's Most Innovative Companies 2014." *Fast Company,* October 7, 2014. http://www.fastcompany.com/3026098/most-innovative-companies-2014/the-worlds-most-innovative-companies-2014 (accessed November 15, 2014).

Sander, Libby. "As Crises Mount, a Push for Communities to Focus on Resilience." *The Chronicle of Philanthropy* 27, no. 3 (November 2014).

Schwab, Charles. *The Age of Independent Advice: The Remarkable History of the Independent Advisor Industry.* San Francisco: Charles Schwab Corp., 2007.

Silverblatt, Robb. "Are There Too Many Mutual Funds?" *US News,* "Money," June 10, 2013 http://money.usnews.com/money/personal-finance/mutual-funds/articles/2013/06/10/are-there-too-many-mutual-funds (accessed November 20, 2014).

Slezak, Steven. "GM's Risk Management Failures Provide Lessons for Other Firms." Globalriskinsights.com, March 14, 2014. http://globalriskinsights.com/2014/03/gms-risk-management-failures-provide-example-for-other-firms/ (accessed November 23, 2014).

Stimson, Daniel. "Inner Workings of the Magnanimous Mind." National Institutes of Health, April 4, 2007. http://www.ninds.nih.gov/news_and_events/news_articles /brain_activity_during_altruism.htm (accessed November 14, 2014).

Sullivan, Paul. "The Folklore of Finance: Beliefs that Contribute to Investors' Failure." *New York Times,* November 15, 2014. http://www.nytimes.com/2014/11/15/your -money/decision-making-methods-obstruct-path-to-investment-goals.html?_r=0 (accessed November 20, 2014).

Tabasco. http://www.tabasco.com/mcilhenny-company/about/ (accessed November 15, 2014).

Thompson, Kendra. "Wealth Transfer: Why It's a More Timely Topic Now than Ever Before." *Accenture,* April 23, 2014. www.accenture.com/us-en/blogs/accenture -wealth-and-asset-management-blog/archive/2014/04/17/wealth-transfer-why-its-a -more-timely-topic-now-than-ever-before.aspx (accessed November 16, 2014).

"Those Medici." *The Economist,* December 23, 1999. http://www.economist.com /node/347333 (accessed November 20, 2014).

"The Transfer of Trust: Wealth and Succession in a Changing World." *Barclays Wealth Insights,* 2011. http://wealth.barclays.com/content/dam/bwpublic/americas/documents/ wealth_management/insights14-the-transfer-of-trust-BWA.pdf (accessed November 9, 2014).

Tough, Paul. *How Children Succeed.* New York: Houghton Mifflin Harcourt, 2012.

Upbin, Bruce. "The Six Habits of Successful Private Companies." *Forbes Magazine,* June 30, 2013. http://www.forbes.com/sites/bruceupbin/2013/06/30/the-six-habits -of-successful-private-companies/ (accessed October 22, 2014).

Visscher, Francois M. de. "Seven Habits of Highly Effective Companies." UMass Amherst Family Business Center, 2014. http://www.umass.edu/fambiz/articles/ money_issues/seven_habits.html (accessed November 20, 2014).

Weinmann, Karlee, and Aimee Groth. "The Ten Largest Family Businesses in America." *Business Insider,* November 17, 2011. http://www.businessinsider.com/the-10-largest- family-businesses-in-America-2011-11?op=1 (accessed October 28, 2014).

Williams, Roy, and Vic Preisser. *Preparing Heirs: Five Steps to a Successful Transition of Family Wealth and Values.* San Francisco: Robert Reed, 2003.

"Working at UPS: Benefits." UPS website. https://ups.managehr.com/benefits.htm (accessed November 5, 2014).

"The World's Most Admired Companies." *Fortune,* March 17, 2014. http://fortune. com/worlds-most-admired-companies/apple-1/ (accessed November 20, 2014).

"The Worst Business Decisions of All Time." 24/7wallst.com, October 17, 2012. http://247wallst.com/special-report/2012/10/17/the-worst-business-decisions-of-all- time/ (accessed November 20, 2014).

Zak, Paul J. "The Moral Molecule: Neuroscience and Economic Behavior." *Psychology Today,* September 8, 2011. http://www.psychologytoday.com/blog/the-moral-mole- cule, (accessed November 14, 2014).

Zynczak, Heather. "Going Global: 4 Major Management Challenges and How to Cope." LinkedIn,March 25,2014.http://www.linkedin.com/today/post/article/20140325200143- 1687653-going-global-4-major-management-challenges-and-how-to-cope?trk=mp- reader-card (accessed November 9, 2014).

Index